Russophobia

How Western Media Turns Russia Into the Enemy

By Dominic Basulto

For Lilia, Helena and Emilio

Russophobia - A diverse spectrum of negative feelings, dislikes, fears, aversion, derision and/or prejudice of Russia, Russians and/or Russian culture.

- Wikipedia (2015)

Contents

Introduction

If you buy into the traditional Western media narrative, then the two former superpowers – the U.S. and Russia – are once again mired in a new, more dangerous Cold War that never really ended. 25 years after the dissolution of the old Soviet Union, Russia is once again Enemy #1 for the U.S. Pentagon and many U.S. politicians.

According to this media narrative, Vladimir Putin is an authoritarian leader bent on reclaiming the former imperial glory of the Soviet Union – first in Ukraine, then in the Baltic States and elsewhere in the post-Soviet space. In doing so, says the conventional wisdom, he is backed by a new wave of nationalism, conservatism and anti-Americanism that has taken hold in Russia.

As a result, Russian intervention anywhere in the world – and especially in Ukraine or Syria – is filled with all kinds of menacing interpretations. In this climate of uncertainty, even information or culture, warns Kremlin critic Peter Pomerantsev, has the potential to be "weaponized" as both sides attempt to gain the upper hand in the geopolitical conflict.

And, more disturbingly, any effort to counter this traditional Western media narrative by a new surge of Russian media abroad is usually immediately derided as "propaganda." Any U.S. scholar who dares to challenge this narrative is immediately branded a "stooge of the Kremlin." And any journalist who dares to question the prevailing logic in the Western media is deemed a "Kremlin mouthpiece."

But is it possible that these Western media narratives are missing something?

In other words, maybe Russia is not the enemy it's made out to be by the media.

That's the overriding thesis of this book, which explores how Western media narratives about Russia profoundly influence the way we think about Russia. These media narratives have important policy implications for the U.S., since it's exactly these narratives and stereotypes that can take on a life of their own when politicians adapt them for their own narrow interests.

Witness the current 2016 U.S. presidential campaign, where Vladimir Putin and Russia make for easy targets for any politician hoping to score points against the Democrats and the Obama administration. That's because most U.S. foreign policy strategies arise from domestic policy considerations, not the other way around. From this perspective, beating up on Russia is a convenient way to beat up on Obama.

Moreover, it's not just that these Western media narratives are often clumsily cartoonish in their attempt to portray Russia as a modern incarnation of the old Evil Empire of the Soviet era – it's that these Western media narratives about Russia have existed for more than 150 years. It's a cyclical process, in which narratives about a "good" Russia typically coincide with periods of Russian weakness, and narratives about a "bad" Russia typically coincide with periods of Russian assertiveness.

Taking a historical perspective, dating back to the turn of the 20th century, American political cartoonists and op-ed writers have always demonized Russia as "the other." In such a way, argues

Moscow scholar Victoria Zhuravleva, Russia has come to represent the polar opposite of what America represents, especially when it comes to defining the differences between the values of the two nations.

There has always been a duality between West and East, Democracy and Authoritarianism, Freedom and Slavery, Liberty and Tyranny, Light and Dark, Good and Evil, and Civilization and Barbarism.

Guess which side Russia usually ends up on?

That's why today's media narratives about Russia are so easy to embrace – they have been honed over more than a century and are timeless, indeed, almost mythical in their content. They are central to both American identity and Russian identity.

And, to make these themes evident to their readers and viewers, Western media typically portrays Russian leaders as the "dark twins" of their American counterparts - which is why the current relationship between Obama and Putin is so fascinating to watch unfold. They are becoming "dark twins" of each other, with their ideologically driven views of the world encompassing polar opposites of the same concepts.

Take, for example, the recent speeches to the 70th annual UN General Assembly in New York by U.S. President Barack Obama and Russian President Vladimir Putin in September 2015. Both took the same floor on the same day in front of the same audience to offer their view of global security, and without mentioning either country by name, managed to take very clear potshots at how their rival views the world.

It made for compelling, must-watch TV (that is, if you enjoy watching live UN webcasts) – two "dark twins" squaring off on the world stage, expressing their view of Good and Evil, Civilization and Barbarism, Freedom and Slavery.

Even Russia watchers in the Western media agreed that, in broad brushstrokes, these two speeches were remarkably similar in content and meaning. As Julia Ioffe of *Foreign Policy* pointed out, "What struck me, however, was how similar the two men sounded and how they used many of the same words and concepts to accuse each other of undermining the very same words and concepts."

This would seem to suggest that, theoretically, there is some common ground for the two nations to unite against a common enemy: ISIS. And, yet, the U.S. and Russia now appear to be further apart in their world view than at any time in the past decade, and perhaps, at any time since the waning days of the Cold War.

U.S. domestic politics, if it follows on its current trajectory, could soon widen that gap even further, by forcing American presidential candidates to take increasingly more assertive stances on what to do about Russia.

In some small way, then, this book hopes to prevent that from happening – to prevent what is now just a "war of words" and an "information war" from escalating into a far more dangerous military confrontation. This is vitally important - not just for the people of the U.S. and Russia, but also for people across the entire planet.

Information War

"These Russians, who confound the appearance with the reality, are trained bears, the sight of which inclines me to regret the wild ones; they have not yet become polished men, although they are spoiled savages."

- Marquis de Custine, *Empire of the Tsar: A Journey Through Eternal Russia* (1839)

Russia is not the enemy

Everywhere you look in the Western mainstream media, there seems to be a chorus of voices suggesting that Russia is the enemy. In the U.S., Republican presidential candidates score points during live television debates by turning Vladimir Putin into a punching bag. President Obama won't even talk face-to-face with Putin unless he's publicly shamed into doing so. The West continues to exclude Russia from its exclusive clubs, including the G8. Meanwhile, the Pentagon is busily re-working its military doctrine to make Russia Enemy #1.

There's just one thing wrong with all of this: Russia is not the enemy.

In a powerful September 2015 op-ed for the *Boston Globe*, Stephen Kinzer, a visiting fellow at the Watson Institute for International Studies at Brown University, makes that point clearly and succinctly. He argues that Washington policymakers are caught up in a Cold War time warp, in which a bipolar confrontation with Russia is "strangely comforting" in a world that seems to have gone off the rails with ISIS, radical Islamist extremism, and a massive influx of Middle East refugees to Europe:

"Having Russia as an enemy is strangely comforting to Americans. It reassures us that the world has not really changed," he writes. "That means we do not have to change our policies. Our back-to-the-future hostility toward Russia allows us to pull out our dusty Cold War playbook. We have resurrected not just that era's anti-

Moscow policies but also the hostile rhetoric that accompanied them."

Where Washington policymakers have failed, he argues, is in attempting to fall back into the same routines and ideas that characterized the Cold War era. That means more spending on conventional military spending, an armed faceoff between NATO and Russia in Europe, and competition for proxy control in places such as Syria.

"Most leading figures in the American political and security establishments grew up during the Cold War," Kinzer notes. "They spent much of their lives believing that the Antichrist lived in Moscow. Today they speak as if the Cold War never ended."

Could it be, then, that the West has failed to frame the Russia problem correctly?

As Kinzer notes in his op-ed, Western triumphalism after the end of the Cold War led many to believe that the West could forever prevent Russia from once again asserting its power in the world.

"Stunned into paralysis by the collapse of the Soviet Union, and without any power to resist, Russians had to watch helplessly as NATO, their longtime enemy, established bases directly on their borders," details Kinzer. "Many in Washington believed that the United States had permanently broken Russian power. In their jubilation, they imagined that we would be able to keep our foot on Russia's neck forever. [...] That was highly unrealistic. By pressing our advantage too strongly in the years after the Cold War, we guaranteed a nationalist reaction."

It's not just Stephen Kinzer who warns about falling into the "new Cold War" trap. Princeton professor emeritus Stephen F. Cohen has warned long and often about ways that the West has failed to take into account Russia's strategic interests, especially in the post-Soviet space. Simply stated, the post-Cold War security architecture of the world had not changed to account for tectonic changes in geopolitical power that occurred with the breakup of the old Soviet Union.

In a bipolar world controlled by two superpowers armed to the teeth with nuclear weapons, Russia was the enemy. There was a clear ideological confrontation between two sides, an Iron Curtain separating Russia from the West, and proxy wars fought on every continent for global dominance.

That's not the case anymore. There's now a multipolar world where economic might, not nuclear might, is the primary attribute of a great power. Instead of Communism, the new ideological threat is ISIS extremism. Economic integration projects have replaced military blocs as the way to attract allies and win over friends.

What has to happen, to one degree or another, is coming to grips with the notion of "Russian aggression." While it's clear that Russia has played a destabilizing role in Ukraine – and, indeed, in much of the post-Soviet space - it's not so clear whether that was simply a result of Russian yearning to reclaim imperial glory and restore the Soviet Union. Perhaps it was a panicked response to what Russia saw as dangerous, menacing moves from the West along its unprotected underbelly?

In an interview with *The National Interest* in August 2015, Henry Kissinger noted that the crisis in Crimea happened just a week after the conclusion of the Sochi Winter Olympics – a huge $50 billion project in which Russia attempted to showcase to the world its efforts to become a trusted member of the global community. From this perspective, the timing of the Crimea crisis is bewildering:

"It is not conceivable that Putin spends sixty billion euros on turning a summer resort into a winter Olympic village in order to start a military crisis the week after a concluding ceremony that depicted Russia as a part of Western civilization," says Kissinger.

So why did Russia make the decision to put its "little green men" into Ukraine?

Even in 2015, there's perhaps no better way to understand Russia's view of modern geopolitics than to watch Vladimir Putin's legendary "Munich Speech" from 2007 in which he outlined all the ways that American superpower dominance was inherently destabilizing and dangerous. In the speech, Putin claimed that American ability to project "hyper force" anywhere in the world and the creation of a unipolar world controlled by one superpower was actually leading to more conflicts and more regional crises – none of them with any kind of political solution.

The real tragedy in all this, as Kinzer suggests, is that America may end up transforming Russia from an "imagined" enemy into a "real" enemy as the result of events already set into motion. It's relatively easy to hypothesize a scenario in which the armed conflict in Ukraine continues to escalate further, with each new escalation moving Russia and the West to a disastrous military confrontation that neither side really wants.

Why Russophobia is so dangerous

The current Russophobia in the Western media should not come as a big surprise. During the Cold War era, the stereotype of dour, unsmiling Russians victimized by a ruthless, authoritarian regime that posed an existential nuclear threat to the West became a mainstay of the media narrative. What images of the Soviet Union that did exist at the time typically showed unsmiling babushkas, Russians standing in queues in front of empty store shelves, and old, crusty Communist apparatchiks pining for the good old days of Joseph Stalin.

From there, unfortunately, Russia's image has only gone downhill.

With the breakup of the Soviet Union, the sudden appearance of American-style capitalism in the country led to a whole new range of Russian character stereotypes that could be assimilated into the Western media narrative – the mafia gangster, the corrupt oligarch spending his ill-gotten gains, the seedy prostitute, and the assorted stock villains attempting to scheme and spend their way to power in the New Russia.

And Hollywood has been all too ready to embrace this Russophobia. In 1985, at the peak of the Cold War, the figure of the boxer Ivan Drago (played by Dolph Lundgren) in "Rocky IV" became a symbol of the menacing military might of the Soviet Union. Just one year earlier, the 1984 film "Red Dawn" portrayed a surprise Soviet attack in Colorado – the ultimate "little green men" scenario, this time exported to American soil. And, of course, more subtly, there were the famous cartoon characters of Boris and Natasha in "Rocky and Bullwinkle."

Even the end of the Cold War hasn't been kind to American perceptions of Russians. The morally bankrupt Russian villain, usually with unsavory links to the Russian criminal underworld, has become a stock character in Hollywood films. Take, for example, David Cronenberg's 2007 film "Eastern Promises," which introduced the world to Russian criminal tattoos and unleashed even more Russian stereotypes into the Western media narrative.

As Mark Hay of GOOD Magazine points out about the film, "Despite having a number of complex characters, and Russians fulfilling (anti-) heroic, villainous, and murky roles, no matter what part they play, the movie's Russians are uniformly surly, besotted, and suspicious."

Even when Hollywood began to make events in Russia part of the plotline (mostly to sell more box office tickets abroad), things didn't go so smoothly, usually involving crafty, manipulative villains in suits doing very bad things. Take, for example, Kenneth Branagh's character in "Jack Ryan: Shadow Recruit," who has some nasty, vindictive surprises to unleash on the American financial system. Almost without exception, Russian characters in Hollywood are spies, contract killers, assassins, pimps, prostitutes or mobsters.

And these stereotypes continue to filter down into other aspects of American pop culture, making them even harder to correct. As a result of this Russophobia, Americans are more likely to believe that Russians pose a risk to the world order. The whole Russian system appears to be in a state of perpetual crisis, brought on by surly, thug-like leaders who disdain Western values. No wonder comic Dan Soder has done an entire standup comedy routine around the notion that "Russians are the scariest white people."

It's no surprise, then, that the American political establishment is starting to buy into this hysteria about Russia. For American politicians, Putin is the perfect Bond villain: unsmiling, unpredictable, egocentric and capable of wiping out the entire free world with the push of a single button.

But you can't just blame the legacy of the Cold War for Russophobia. Ever since Westerners started making trips to nineteenth century imperial Russia, Russophobia has been a key part of the Western narrative about Russia. Starting in the 1820s, Britain – concerned by Russia's defeat of Napoleonic France - began to inject elements of Russophobia into any discussion of the growing Russian empire.

As a result, for nearly 200 years, the vast Russian motherland has always been described as a backwards land, filled with a mixed-race, sub-European people who failed to experience the Enlightenment as the result of being under the Mongol yoke for so long. It's no wonder that Western historians continue to write about Russia's strange love-hate relationship with European civilization.

In 1839, the French aristocrat Marquis de Custine, writing about his three months of travel in the imperial Russia of Tsar Nicholas I, came back shaking his head about what he had just witnessed in St. Petersburg, Moscow and Yaroslavl. In "Empire of the Tsar: A Journey Through Eternal Russia," he mocked the obsequious flattery of the Tsarist court, the constant spying, the backwardness of the Russian Orthodox Church and the desperate (and ill-fated) attempts by the Russian nobility to acquire even a thin veneer of European civilization.

It wouldn't be overstating matters to say that the "de Tocqueville of Russia" was Patient Zero of the West's Russophobia. Some of the passages from the Marquis de Custine's book are tough to stomach, as he outlines all the ways that Russian civilization is inferior to European civilization. As he saw it, Russia could never become part of the European world, no matter how hard it tried. The members of Russia's aristocracy had "just enough of the gloss of European civilization to be spoiled as savages but not enough to become cultivated men... They were like trained bears who made you long for the wild ones."

Fast forward 175 years, and it's possible to see the same sentiments echoed almost exactly in the sentiments of American diplomats. In 2014, U.S. Secretary of State John Kerry famously noted that Russia was pursuing a nineteenth century strategy in a twenty-first century world, preferring aggressive military action to the more civilized recourse of international law. In doing so, Kerry was essentially ripping a page out of the travelogue of the Marquis de Custine:

"I don't reproach the Russians for being what they are; what I blame them for is their desire to appear to be what we [Europeans] are... They are much less interested in being civilized than in making us believe them so...," writes de Custine. They would be quite content to be in effect more awful and barbaric than they actually are, if only others could thereby be made to believe them better and more civilized."

In 1911, the American journalist and author Ambrose Bierce satirically summarized the prevailing view of Russia in *The Devil's Dictionary* with a caustic description of Russians: "Russian, noun. A person with a Caucasian body and a Mongolian soul. A Tartar emetic." In other words, a Russian might look like a Westerner on the outside, but inside, it's a whole different ballgame. There are influences from Mongolia and the vast Russian steppe, a mix of ethnicities and a distinctly Eurasian worldview.

Giving the immense social upheaval surrounding the 1917 Bolshevik Revolution and the rise of Stalin, perceptions began to grow, as Alan Cowell has pointed out in the *New York Times*, that Russia was "an inscrutable and menacing land that plays by its own rules." In 1939, Winston Churchill famously remarked that Russia is "a riddle, wrapped in a mystery, inside an enigma." And that's a perception that's lasted for more than 50 years, especially after the Soviet Union pulled down the Iron Curtain in 1945 and separated itself from the Western world.

In 1945, just as the world was dividing into two armed camps of superpowers, the prevailing view of Russia was that it was an inferior land filled with a mixed race of people who were not quite Europeans and not quite Asians. This, said U.S. General George S. Patton, made them particularly dangerous:

"The difficulty in understanding the Russian is that we do not take cognizance of the fact that he is not a European, but an Asiatic, and therefore thinks deviously. We can no more understand a Russian than a Chinaman or a Japanese, and from what I have seen of them, I have no particular desire to understand them, except to ascertain how much lead or iron it takes to kill them. In addition to his other Asiatic characteristics, the Russian have no regard for human life and is an all out son of bitch, barbarian, and chronic drunk."

Yes, there is something impenetrable about Russia. This vast country stretching across 12 time zones is somehow a blend of West and East, exotic, mysterious and just a bit menacing. The nation seems to be perpetually under the iron thumb of an authoritarian regime, buffeted regularly by controversy, coups and revolutions.

Within Russia, there have always been Slavophiles and Westernizers, both seeking to take Russia in opposite directions. And, standing in the heart of the Eurasian landmass, Russia has become famously xenophobic about the threat posed by foreign invaders. It's easy to understand why: Napoleonic France, Nazi Germany and the Mongols have to be just about the perfect trifecta of xenophobia-inducing foreign invaders.

And, now 70 years after the end of the Great Patriotic War, Russia sees itself once again encircled by the West as some kind of vast geopolitical conspiracy. It sees its traditional values under pressure from the West, its diplomatic principles continually rebuked by the West, and its worldview derided as belonging to an earlier century. More importantly, it sees its very borders under threat from the West, given the continued eastward expansion of NATO to the very doorstep of Russia.

The problem now is that both Russia and the West have conflicting views on the causes and consequences of international events. Whereas the West sees the world as progressing towards an enlightened form of liberal democracy, in which nations must be set free to experience the richness and goodness of modernity, Russia sees the need to restore the sovereignty of nations. As Russia sees it, nations must be helped to keep the chaos and anarchy of the world at bay.

The danger is that political leaders within Russia and the U.S. are starting to develop a binary view of the world: good or evil, right or wrong. Whereas ideology was never part of the debate in the post-Cold War world - the whole world appeared to be hurtling towards the "end of history" – ideology is now once again becoming part of how Russia and the West views the world. Not surprisingly, we are starting to see the same type of zero-sum thinking that we saw during the Cold War. Complex geopolitical events are oversimplified, reduced to this binary view of the world.

That's why Russophobia is so dangerous – it starts with the baseline assumption that Russia is evil, backwards and barbaric. Any attempt by Russia to change this narrative within the Western media is derided as mere propaganda. And any attempts by Russia to take specific actions to influence the course of events within this narrative – Ukraine and Syria are the clearest examples - are seen, at best, as attempts to co-opt the West, and at worst, as dangerous aggression that must be punished.

Is there a way to shift this narrative and find a way to cure the West of its Russophobia? Let's hope so. An inability by the West to accept Russia as an equal power with its own interests in the world is only going to destabilize the global order and lead to a state of permanent crisis.

The 'Blame Russia' game hurts the West more than Russia

The more Russia is viewed as the "global villain," the more pressure the West will face to ratchet up its policy responses to perceived Russian aggression. At what point, though, will both sides run out of any good options?

Ever since the escalation of the Ukraine crisis in March 2014, the "Blame Russia" campaign has been in overdrive. It's not just that the West blames Russia for the escalating crisis in Ukraine, it's that the West blames Russia for practically anything that goes wrong in the world. That relentless attempt to portray Russia as the global villain, however, could backfire.

Here's how the "Blame Russia" game works - pick any bad news in the world and immediately try to find a nefarious Russian connection behind it. Bonus points if this "nefarious Russian connection" involves Vladimir Putin, the Russian intelligence services (e.g. the FSB, successor to the KGB), evil Russian hackers, or wacky Russian nationalists.

In the past year, Russia has been blamed (at least indirectly) for the outbreak of the Ebola virus, for the tragic explosion of a U.S. space rocket, and even for the escalating cost of hosting the Winter Olympics – not to mention the escalation of the crisis in Syria and the unleashing of chaos in the Middle East.

However, the "Blame Russia" strategy might force the West into disastrous policy moves that could end up hurting it as well. The reason is that the illogic of the "Blame Russia" game has been pushed to such a point that it's led to a very real paranoia of Russia

– and that forces the hand of Western governments. The more that Russia is presented as the unruly bear migrating away from its native taiga, the more that Western governments have to act to preserve their own reputations.

There are now three very concrete examples of how the West's "Blame Russia" strategy is leading to some very ill advised steps by Western governments.

The first example is economic sanctions. We know from historical experience that a "sanctions war" (as they refer to it in Russia) is only going to lead to a race to the economic bottom. You ban their financial assets, and they ban your fruits and vegetables. You try to sink the Russian ruble, and they come up with a "de-dollarization" plan for the global economy. You cut off their credit, and they cut off your gas.

The second example is the new call for a military buildup by NATO, driven by fears that Russia will make land grabs in the Baltic States, or in Scandinavia, in Moldova, elsewhere in Ukraine or just about anywhere in the post-Soviet space. Yellow submarines spotted off the coast of Sweden? They must be Russian nuclear subs preparing for a surprise strike on Scandinavia. More "little green men" spotted in Ukraine? They must be planning to carve a land bridge through Ukraine, from Russia to Crimea.

George Soros is even calling on European nations to "wake up" and wreck their own economies with a multi-billion-dollar military buildup to counter recent moves by Russia in Europe. Soros says Russia now poses an "existential threat" to Europe.

The third example is the West refusing to coordinate counter-terrorism responses with Russia on ISIS, even as jihadist extremism shows signs of coming to the U.S. and Canada. The West has always treated terrorism differently when it happened in Russia - Beslan was initially viewed by the West as Russia's 9/11 – and that has led to a policy blind spot now that events in Iraq and Syria have spiraled out of control. Soon it may be too late for anyone to do something about jihadist extremism in the Middle East.

And you can already see the next policy steps that the West will be forced to make, now that Russia has been cast as the "global villain." In areas ranging from space exploration to nuclear nonproliferation, there is no longer any political will to find any common ground with Russia. Now that the Republicans have regained control of the U.S. Congress after big midterm wins in November 2014, destructive political moves – such as providing lethal, military assistance to Ukraine – might actually have a chance of passing, with or without Barack Obama's consent. In a best-case scenario, we'll be in a holding pattern until the end of the 2016 presidential election.

In a world divided into two armed camps, a "Blame Russia" strategy might have worked. But in a world that's globalized, fast and flat, a country like Russia has options. Moreover, when actions used to punish Russia (such as financial sanctions) don't work as planned, it only produces the image of a "shrinking hegemon" forced to ratchet up its policy response out of reputational needs. In other words, the West has to start matching deeds to rhetoric - otherwise it looks weak.

Complicating matters is that Russia now feels that it has been boxed into a corner. Today for Russia, it is very difficult to allay Western suspicions and rollback economic sanctions, and that's leading to some pretty erratic responses from the Kremlin. Having Russian fighter planes and bombers buzz Europe is probably not the best way to quell any growing paranoia in the West.

The race to the bottom intensifies the more the blame piles up, but don't tell that to the mainstream Western media. The job of 21st century journalism is the same as the job of 19th century journalism -- sell newspapers and magazines. The way to do that is by placing an unsmiling Vladimir Putin with dark sunglasses on the cover – the classic Hollywood bad guy, the "pariah," the evil genius with his hands on the nuclear button, capable of acting everywhere and nowhere at once.

Unfortunately for the West, this story may not end like the classic Hollywood blockbuster, with the villain vanquished, the world saved, and the heroes embracing against the backdrop of a rising sun. This may end up being more of a neo-noir thriller, with complicated plot twists, strange characters acting erratically, and a final ending that satisfies nobody.

The West's pop culture propaganda war

The positive message that the West once offered to Russia during the waning days of the Cold War—democracy, freedom, respect for human dignity—has been replaced by a starkly negative message that encourages confrontation rather than engagement. Instead of telling Russians how great things are in America, the new strategy seems to be telling Russians how terrible things are in their own country. In the lexicon of political campaigns, America is going negative.

As a result, for many in the West, Russia has become a cartoon evil empire. According to this logic, everything in Russia is crap, everywhere in Russia is cold and bleak, and every Russian—young or old—is either stupid or poor (but usually both). And anyone who would lead that type of nation must be an autocratic, authoritarian thug. Because, logic.

Take, for example, Louis C.K.'s standup comedy routine about Russia that went viral in 2015. It's a 10-minute laugh fest about his miserable, nihilistic vacation to post-Soviet Russia. He starts off by commenting on how stupid the Russians were for building Moscow in the middle of a forest, and then proceeds to reel off a litany of things that are depressing about Russia—mysterious waiters that sell you black market Coca-Cola, nasty little urchins that roam the streets at night and details about the physically daunting layout of Moscow (including super-wide thoroughfares to make sure missiles can get to and from Red Square and subway stations that seem to descend endlessly to an underworld below).

Now, take a deep breath and ask yourself the following question: If a Russian comedian were to deliver this same kind of comic routine about America, wouldn't it immediately be hailed as an example of the hate-filled propaganda speech filling Russian TV airwaves these days?

In general, the West seems to be lost in a sort of time warp, never having really adjusted to the dissolution of the old Soviet Union. The same stock characters and ideas that were popular 25 years ago during the peak of the Cold War are now reappearing as part of an undeclared pop culture-fueled propaganda war with Russia.

Look no further than the character of Olya Povlatsky on NBC's "Saturday Night Live"—a bitter, dirt-poor Russian woman (or is she Ukrainian?) who complains about everything in modern Russia. She's wickedly funny, but she's also a stock character out of the Cold War era, when Russians queued up for life's essentials just about every day.

Not convinced about that time warp issue? Watch Louis C.K.'s comic routine—he suggests that the past 25 years in Russia have essentially been one, unbroken chain of misery. Getting the exact date right is not even important because Russia, the Soviet Union, what's the difference?

"But anyway, I went to Russia in 19—, no, 20—no, when the f**k was it?—yes, 1994. I went to Russia. It has just become Russia again," says Louis C.K. "It was the Soviet Union until really that year, everything started to crash down."

Sadly, the people who should be leading the charge in America's "information war" with Russia—politicians, diplomats, professors and think tank experts—have largely been co-opted by America's pop culture creative class—filmmakers, actors, musicians and, yes, comedians such as Jon Stewart, John Oliver and Stephen Colbert. Bad jokes about Russia and funny "Simpsons" characters have replaced any type of meaningful engagement with Russia.

Want to do a withering critique of Russian state-owned TV propaganda? There's no need to do a thorough academic study— if you're the *New York Times*, just sign up comic writer Gary Shteyngart and pay him to sit in front of multiple TVs watching Russian news and entertainment for a week in a swank Manhattan hotel. And then give the piece an absurd title that's just the right mix of sarcasm, irony and humor: "Out of my mouth comes unimpeachable manly truth."

Want to make a statement about Russia's human rights violations? Sign up HBO to make a documentary about Pussy Riot. Or, better yet, get Madonna to adopt the girls of Pussy Riot as a new cultural signifier of her hipness and commitment to human rights.

At some point, the West stopped trying to appeal to the real, everyday people in Russia with a positive message of hope. Instead, it focused on trying to appeal to a very slender cross-section of Russia's English-speaking, Western-educated creative class, which it believes is the best wedge to push Putin out of power. The new focus, apparently, is convincing this top one percent of Russians that their nation has become a global laughingstock.

As a result, the West celebrates people like Garry Kasparov, someone who's basically irrelevant in Russia these days. But since he's willing to dish out the West's negative message in a big way, he's embraced on American newspaper op-ed pages.

Who did the *New York Times* sign up to do a withering op-ed critique of Russia just in time for Victory Day in 2015 (one of the most important days of the year for Russians, just behind New Year's and March 8th)? That's right, acclaimed Russian writer Mikhail Shishkin, who wrote a predictably depressing piece about the various ways that Russia's leaders continue to abuse their people and spew hatred abroad:

"It is impossible to breathe in a country where the air is permeated with hatred. Much hatred has always been followed in history by much blood," writes Shishkin. "What awaits my country? Transformation into a gigantic version of Ukraine's eastern Donbass region? [...] Once again, the dictatorship is calling on its subjects to defend the homeland, mercilessly exploiting the propaganda of victory in the Great Patriotic War. Russia's rulers have stolen my people's oil, stolen their elections, stolen their country. And stolen their victory."

Want to really get inside the heads of Russian intellectuals? Tell them that their proud heritage of having the world's greatest literature is going down the tubes, as Owen Matthews recently wrote for *Foreign Policy* in his piece "Is Russian Literature Dead?" The demise of Russian literature is all part of an overall cultural rot in Russia, he implies.

Again, more negative messaging, because that's what works. Just ask any political consultant.

However, a lot has changed since the old days of the Cold War, something the West seems to have forgotten. At the end of the day, the reason why the West may lose the "information war" (and some would say, the "disinformation war") with Russia is because it's still stuck in the 1980s Cold War era mindset. It's tone-deaf to new changes and attitudes emerging in Russia. It can't see the ways in which a global, multilateral world is changing. And, most importantly, the messaging from the West has just become so negative. You simply can't win by going negative over and over again for 25 years.

Ever wonder why folks like Vladimir Putin come to power in Russia? It's hard not to see how more than a decade of being made the butt of Western jokes gets a bit stale. It's simply impossible for so much bad news and misery to come out of a single country on such a consistent basis.

And, as Louis C.K. would say, that's all I got.

Fear and loathing in Sochi

Still not convinced that the Western media has waged an information war against Russia ever since the breakup of the Soviet Union? Just consider the coordinated efforts by the U.S. media to ensure that the 2014 Sochi Winter Olympics would become a $50 billion failure for Russia.

Even before the twin Volgograd terror attacks in southern Russia just days before New Year's 2014, it was almost inevitable that we would see one last spasm of fear and loathing in the Western media before Sochi hosted the Winter Olympics in February.

For more than a year, there had been the constant drumbeat of warnings that Sochi 2014 was going to be the most expensive Olympics in history due to profligate corruption and cronyism. As soon as Sochi put the finishing touches on any new Olympic venue, it was accompanied by horror stories in the media of human rights abuses of migrant workers and impending ecological disasters.

With a nod to Detroit ruin porn, you can call this Sochi disaster porn.

Case in point: a cover story from *Bloomberg Businessweek* in early 2014, which depicts a badass-looking Russian Mafioso bear armed to the hilt and holding a riot shield with the simple question: "Is Russia Ready?" Not that there was really going to be any attempt to answer this question in a rational way within the magazine itself.

You knew the answer even before you opened the issue — the story was going to be about boycotts, terrorism, waster, greed and cronyism. That's what sells magazines these days. The editors told you as much with a behind-the-scenes look at how the cover got made.

This cover story in *Bloomberg Businessweek* had plenty of predecessors in the burgeoning field of Sochi disaster porn. Just a few days earlier, the *Los Angeles Times* asked, "Are the Sochi Olympics Heading for Disaster? Columnists and bloggers were making a last-minute plea to move the Winter Olympics somewhere else — anywhere else! — just so Sochi couldn't host them.

Even what should have been warm-and-fuzzy photo essays about Sochi started off with a warning: "Islamist insurgents, tough Cossacks and warm winters – welcome to Russia's Olympic host city."

A front-page story in the *New York Times* on December 18, 2013 on the Olympic Torch Relay reveled in the fact that the Olympic Torch had gone out repeatedly on its 123-day journey across Russia (including one incident where it was re-lit ignominiously with a cigarette lighter). The title was link-bait everywhere for the Sochi haters: "Got a Light? Torch Relay Seems Cursed to the Ends of the Earth."

Of course it was cursed, because this was Russia!

If you're the *New York Times*, don't focus on the fact that the Olympic Torch would go on a spacewalk into outer space travel to the North Pole — or that it would travel 40,000 miles across

Russia and feature 14,000 people in a massive, national unifying run-up to the Winter Olympics. That doesn't sell newspapers.

The gold standard of Sochi disaster porn, of course, was a massive, 400-page tome on Sochi published to coincide with the Winter Games called "An Atlas of War and Tourism in the Caucasus." The cover features a 29-year-old stripper from a local Sochi hotel rolling around with an animal on what looks like a red harem bed. If you take off the cover jacket of the book, you still can't escape the fear and loathing — there is a quote from Vladimir Putin that is meant to be both ironic and sarcastic, "The Olympic family is going to feel at home in Sochi."

It's sarcastic, you see, because the entire 400-page tome is filled with despicable images that make you cringe — burned-out buildings, ugly people, and post-apocalyptic scenes out of a war zone. It's so bad, in fact, that this book of Sochi disaster porn is no longer welcome in Russia, and certainly not in Sochi.

So a casual observer might ask: Why does all this Sochi disaster porn exist? The same questions have been asked about Detroit ruin porn — what purpose does it really serve other than to rack up page views from the haters?

The knee-jerk reaction, of course, is to chalk it up to the long, strange, disaster-plagued history of Russia. Consider that the greatest novel that Russia has ever produced — "*Anna Karenina*" — ends with the heroine throwing herself on the train tracks in suicide. Do you know of any Russian book that has a happy ending? Even within Russia, people are resigned to their nation's cosmic fate and are ever wary of any leader promising hope and a new way to the future.

Except that there seems to be something more profound and interesting happening here that goes beyond just a massive Cold War hangover in the West. Even when Russia attempts to do what the Western media wants it to do — build a democracy, privatize the economy, let loose the dissenters — it's met with more fear and loathing.

Putin's "Christmas Surprise" of granting amnesty to jailed oil oligarch Khodorkovsky and Pussy Riot? *A cynical PR move ahead of Sochi.* Russia stepping away from the Euromaidan mess in Ukraine? *A nefarious diplomatic bargaining trick with a hidden agenda.* Russia's colorful "Rainbow" uniforms for the Sochi 2014 Olympics? *A cynical attempt to co-opt the LGBT boycott movement.* Quite simply, in the Western media's eyes, Russia could do nothing right when it came to the Sochi Olympics.

Perhaps the best explanation for all this is something that Russian historian Victoria Zhuravleva has explained as the role of specific images and myths about Russia in the creation of an American identity. America, you see, needs to demonize Russia as "the other" in order to fulfill its messianic role in the world.

From this perspective, Russia is the "dark twin" of America. Sochi is the enemy, Putin is the stock villain, and all of Putin's Olympic officials are bit players in a huge American morality play. America wants to be able to save Russia from itself. It is the way that it has been for nearly 150 years.

In her book, "Understanding Russia in the United States: Images and Myths 1881-1914," Zhuravleva points out all the examples throughout the history of U.S.-Russian relations where Americans have used cartoons to demonize Russia. Sochi disaster porn, in fact, fits perfectly with this history of American mythmaking about Russia.

Which brings us back to the *Bloomberg Businessweek* story and the cartoon image of the Russian bear. This is exactly what Zhuravleva is talking about. In a series of notes and annotations, the magazine's editors explain how they arrived at the final image of the bear for the cover. First, they start with a stock cartoon image of Russia — the bear. Then, they resort to all the other cultural stereotypes that enforce the standard myths of Russia, including an early sketch of the Russian bear lighting the Olympic torch with a cigarette lighter (later replaced, after the Volgograd terror attacks, by a riot shield).

The alternative cover was just going to feature a bunch of words to characterize Russia: "Boycotts, Cronyism, Terrorism, Waste, Greed." You see, the cover is a giant political cartoon, in the style of all the other American cartoons about Russia over the past 150 years.

The only way Russia could have put an end to this non-stop flow of Sochi disaster porn, of course, was to pull off the most stunning Winter Olympics in history. (Just as Detroit can only put an end to Detroit ruin porn by making the city amazing again.) Russia needed to make the Sochi 2014 Winter Olympics so over-the-top enchanting and entertaining that you could even forgive billions of dollars of colossal government waste. It needed to snow everyday, non-stop, so that people could see Sochi as a winter wonderland rather than a subtropical war zone. The TV cameras needed to have global audiences marveling at how the Russians pulled it off.

And, you know what? They did. But they didn't do it in a way that let America still believe in its messianic role in the world.

Russia cannot be understood with the meme alone

As an Olympic volunteer in Russia in 2014, I saw the Sochi Olympics up close and personal. For nearly a month, I lived inside the Sochi Olympic bubble.

NBC may have streamed every moment of every Winter Olympic event as part of its billion-dollar broadcast deal, but I did not watch any of it. Instead, my impressions of Sochi primarily came via interactions with guests visiting the Olympic Park as well as conversations with the Sochi 2014 volunteers working at both the Coastal and Mountain Clusters. Throughout the day, big-screen TVs showed action from around Sochi, while smaller screens at dining halls and cafes carried live Russian TV coverage of the Games.

As a result, I knew when Team Russia snagged its final three medals of the Olympics when my airplane en route from Sochi to Moscow exploded in wild applause as soon as we landed at Sheremetyevo Airport in Moscow.

Likewise, I knew when Team Russia failed in its quest for Olympic hockey gold when my high-speed train to the Mountain Cluster went ghostly silent and the passengers next to me kept hitting the refresh buttons on their smartphone browsers, certain that the final score against Finland had been a cruel mistake.

I could tell which countries were doing well in the overall medals count by the profusion of hats, pins, flags and outrageous outfits that appeared the same day in Sochi's Olympic Park. As long as the Dutch speed skaters piled up medals on a daily basis, it was a safe bet that you would see orange everywhere you walked in the Olympic Park.

Overall, I attended nearly twenty sporting events at every single one of Sochi's new competition venues, with the exception of the new Sanki sliding center where both American and Russian athletes catapulted themselves down the mountain at record-setting speeds. I also saw the Opening Ceremony at Fisht Olympic Stadium and visited every single one of the sponsor pavilions in Sochi's World Fair-style Olympic Park.

I learned a lot living inside Sochi's Olympic bubble.

First of all, the New Russia looks nothing like the Old Russia. This actually wasn't my first time visiting Sochi. My previous visit to Sochi had been in summer 2012, when I vacationed along the Black Sea in the center of Sochi at an old Soviet-era cement block hotel called the Zhemchuzhina ("The Pearl").

It was hard then to imagine how Olympic Sochi might look—people still commuted around the city in Soviet-era buses, hung out at faded-look sanatoriums, and clung to symbols of the Old Russia. Walk 15 minutes from the main Sochi railway station, for example, and you'd run smack dab into a huge mosaic of Vladimir Ilyich Lenin. In the mountains in 2012, there were dusty roads filled with posters for new ski resorts and ski condos, but nothing exactly to see except empty construction pits. That new high-speed train line connecting the Mountain and Coastal Clusters? It hadn't even been built yet.

Fast-forward 18 months, though, and the changes in Sochi were breathtaking. All of the competition venues were beautiful—especially the venues in the Olympic Park such as the Iceberg

Skating Palace, the Bolshoi Ice Dome and Adler Arena when lit up at night. There was a riotous explosion of color as soon as you passed over the Olympic Ring-themed passageway from the Olympic Park rail station into the Olympic Park, home of the Olympic Flame. And that was echoed in the Mountain Cluster, where three world-class ski resorts had been cross-linked and connected with an array of roads, bridges and ski gondolas. At night, Rosa Khutor—Sochi's largest ski resort area designed in the style of a Swiss Alps village—was absolutely beautiful, lit up in pastels and illuminated by fireworks every night.

And what was perhaps most remarkable of all was how the signs and symbols of the New Russia referenced the signs and symbols of the Old Russia. The new clock tower at the Rosa Khutor alpine village was designed to echo the architecture of the old Stalinist-era clock tower at the main railway station in the center of Sochi. The Bolshoi Ice Dome, decorated with Olympic rings, evoked the famous Bolshoi Theater in Moscow. The ambitious new Gorky Gorod in the mountains was bigger and more expansive than the recently refurbished Gorky Park in Moscow, itself one of the few tourist attractions in Russia that Westerners might recognize by name.

Buildings for guests and journalists were named for famous places in Moscow, like Alexandrovskii Sad (the garden next to the Kremlin) and Chistyie Prudyi (the "Clean Ponds" neighborhood in Moscow). Conference rooms at the Main Media Center were named for the likes of Pushkin and Dostoevsky. Even the name of Sochi's large, meandering ski resort valley—Krasnaya Polyana ("Red Meadow")—seemed to evoke the name of Russia's most famous destination—Red Square. (And, for good measure, the central meeting place at Rosa Khutor where all the Olympic concerts took place was called "Rose Square.")

Secondly, I learned that Russia cannot be understood by the meme alone. Even though I was living inside an Olympic Bubble, it was impossible to ignore the social media memes that emerged during the Olympics—everything from #SochiProblems to the Sochi Selfie. You heard the foreign journalists talking about these memes on the media buses that dropped them off at the competition venues around Sochi.

However, talk to any Russian attending the Olympics in the Olympic Park, and you'd probably get a blank look if you mentioned a social media meme like #NightmareBear. That "nightmare" bear was simply the lovable white polar bear Misha, the winter sports-loving cousin of Moscow's famous brown bear mascot from the 1980s Summer Olympics. Misha sang and danced at the Olympic venues during breaks in the action, and posed for photos with children while walking around the Olympic Park. At the Closing Ceremony, Misha famously shed a tear for the closing of the Winter Olympics.

So were these social media memes actually on-point? There is a famous Russian poem by Fyodor Tyutchev that is often used to explain the inscrutability of Russia:

"Russia cannot be understood with the mind alone, No ordinary yardstick can span her greatness: She stands alone, unique – In Russia, one can only believe."

More than 100 years after Tyutchev wrote those lines, you can update that poem to read: "Russia cannot be understood by meme alone." In Sochi, the memes that became popular in the West seemed to be self-fulfilling prophecies of journalists, who came to Russia with a specific image of the nation. Memes, shared via Facebook and Twitter, were meant to infect other visitors to the Olympics with certain stereotypes of Russia before the Games even began—that the nation was somehow incompetent and the people unfriendly.

By the end of the month, though, even the most cynical of the #SochiProblems promoters had to admit that Russia's Olympic organizers were doing their best to improve things on a continual basis. Every day brought new stories of how Sochi's volunteers and paid workers made everyday life easier and more convenient for guests to the Olympic city.

Thirdly, it became increasingly clear that the U.S. has a Canada problem. It was striking at times at how muted the American presence in Sochi felt. At the competition arenas, it seemed like there were a few hardy American fans waving flags, but that was it. You saw the NBC broadcast folks wearing their Nike-designed jackets, or maybe wearing some Team USA Olympic gear, but they were quiet and muted when traversing the Olympic Park.

Maybe this had to do with the official warnings sent to Americans before the Games: Don't wear your colors, don't broadcast that you're an American, don't wear the stars-and-stripes too proudly. The USA House in the Olympic Park was a "private home" and that meant that even American guests weren't welcome unless they were friends and family of the athletes (or one of Team USA's deep-pocketed sponsors). The one attempt I made to hang out at the USA House was greeted with suspicion—after showing my passport, I was allowed to do some Team USA shopping at a boutique featuring Nike and Ralph Lauren Polo, but not allowed into any of the non-commercial areas of the USA House.

Now contrast that approach to the approach of the Canadians at the Games. They were everywhere you looked, draped in red and proudly bearing the Canadian symbol of the maple leaf. At the women's Olympic gold medal hockey game, in which Canada faced off against Team USA, muted chants of "U-S-A" were quickly eclipsed by chants of "Can-a-da." At times, 80 percent of the Bolshoi Ice Dome appeared to be pulling for the Canadians.

Canadians approached you on the streets and at the venues, unafraid to show their pride in making the long journey from Canada to support their team. On sunny days, the Canada House in the Olympic Park was filled with outdoor chairs and Canadians lounging around in the fresh air. Next door, the lawn of the Team USA house was empty, the doors closed, and protected by security guards.

Maybe this Olympic Park experience is just one sample in a huge population of events, but you can read this experience as part of a larger issue: the U.S. has a Canada problem. Whether because of ideology or some other factor, Russians can embrace Canada, but can't embrace the U.S. Americans were on edge when they traveled to Sochi, but the Canadians weren't.

This seems to show up in the foreign policy calculus of Americans when it comes to Russia—they don't trust Russia. Just like the Team USA house in the Olympic Park was sealed off from visitors, it now sometimes feels like the U.S. really doesn't want to interact with the rest of the world, and especially not with Russia. Americans don't mind if Russians buy their Nike and Ralph

Lauren Polo products abroad, but they don't really want to take the time to learn and experience a new culture. And, as we saw in both the Opening and Closing Ceremonies, Russia's is a very rich culture indeed.

Finally, it became obvious that these were Russia's Games as much as Putin's Games. As Russia's medal count soared throughout the Winter Games, making this Russia's best-ever appearance in the Winter Olympics—even including all the powerhouse teams of the combined USSR teams—you could see the pride and Olympic spirit sweeping up Russia.

The first visitors to the Olympic Park walked around in disappointingly small groups, and there seemed to be few foreigners. People initially joked that this was an Olympics for the athletes and the 25,000 or so Sochi 2014 volunteers.

By the end, though, there was a mad rush to see the Olympic Park, if only for a day. Seats began to fill. Long lines stood outside the Bosco Olympic Store at all hours of the day and night. Families came out in droves, clothed in official Russian Olympic gear. Cheers of "Rossiya" ("Russia") emanated everywhere you went, and even the most hardened Russia critics admitted that somehow, despite all odds, Russia had built something special— a place where Russians actually smiled, where athletes set all-time Olympic records at world-class venues, and Russia actually had something worthy of being shared with friends and families that didn't involve antagonizing the West.

Going into the Games, there had been a fear that these would be Putin's Games, a place for Vladimir Putin to show off his version of Russia to the world. Yet, Putin seemed to have a soft touch at the Games—he made one memorable appearance at the USA and Canada Houses at the Olympic Park, and he showed up for the USA-Russia hockey match and at the Iceberg Skating Palace. You heard stories about him popping in to congratulate athletes who had won gold medals, but his image and presence was muted in Sochi. This was a national, shared experience, not an experience of one man or one group of officials.

The Closing Ceremony provided a final, satisfying coda to the end of the Games. For Russia, they turned out to be the most successful Winter Olympics in the nation's history. They helped to introduce a New Russia to the world. They helped to shatter stereotypes about Russia that appeared in the form of persistent social media memes. And they might have helped to unite a country that was at times skeptical and critical of the $50 billion spent to host the Winter Olympics. All of this, of course, would have been impossible to learn if I hadn't been living inside the Sochi Olympic Bubble.

What World Cup 2018 has to do with Sochi 2014

Given this experience with the 2014 Sochi Winter Olympics, it's hard not to see a similar type of political motive behind the decision to call into question Russia's right to host the 2018 World Cup. Calls to boycott the Sochi 2014 Winter Olympics are now being followed by calls to boycott Russia's hosting of the FIFA World Cup in 2018.

As a result, your first reaction after hearing about the FIFA World Cup corruption scandal—a scandal so ugly it could wind up as one of the worst scandals ever in the history of sports—should have been: "Uh-oh, here we go again." After all, the takedown of powerful FIFA officials on corruption, fraud and racketeering charges has the not entirely unthinkable chance of stripping the World Cup from Russia in 2018.

Sound familiar? In many ways, this calling into question Russia's right to host the 2018 World Cup is reminiscent of similar attempts to block Russia from hosting the Winter Olympics in 2014. And that was in 2012–2013, before the appearance of "little green men" in Crimea and the breakout of hostilities in eastern Ukraine, both of which occurred within weeks of the closing ceremonies in Sochi.

In the lead-up to Sochi 2014, it was possible to make the case that the West was actively looking for a way to downplay or otherwise derail Russia's hosting of the Winter Olympics, but was simply lacking a valid geopolitical argument. What the West needed was something similar to the Soviet invasion of Afghanistan, for example, which led to the boycott of the 1980 Moscow Summer Olympics.

As a result, the impetus for the "Boycott Sochi" adventure was based primarily on social and cultural grounds — Russia as an unwelcoming nation for LGBT fans and athletes — and secondarily on Sochi's inability to host the event in the first place (the whole "there's no snow in Sochi" argument). The "terrorism" argument — Sochi being located so close to the violent Caucasus — also played a role.

Ultimately, the attempt to block, boycott and otherwise throw a pall of uncertainty over the Sochi Olympics was a case of too little, too late. By the time the calls began to "Boycott Sochi," it would have been practically impossible to move the Winter Games elsewhere (although Salzburg and Vancouver were more than happy to oblige if necessary).

So you can just imagine how the West is now salivating at the chance of stripping Russia of the 2018 World Cup — or, at the very least, dragging Russia's reputation through the mud and filth of the "FIFA mafia" scandal. In short, the West is now close to having the same geopolitical argument that it had in 1980 — the invasion of Ukraine or the bombing of ISIS in Syria is the new invasion of Afghanistan — to call for a boycott of the World Cup. That's still a dicey proposition — especially because it's tricky to define the crisis in Ukraine as a true "invasion" — so the mafia-like FIFA corruption charges offer a convenient back door.

What makes things so easy for the West — if, indeed, this is a politically motivated attempt by the West to disqualify Russia's World Cup bid — is that Russia's involvement in the FIFA scandal seems to fit a bigger narrative—"Russia as a corrupt country without a respect for the rule of law."

Anyone's who's ever read a story about corrupt Russian oligarchs stashing their cash overseas in secretive bank accounts and running all kinds of scams to launder their ill-gotten gains can easily buy into the idea of Russian World Cup officials also being involved in this scandal.

And, of even greater concern for Russia, this scandal came in May 2015, almost three years before the start of the 2018 World Cup. In other words, there might be time to nullify the Russian bid and hand it over to someone else. The Brits, already locked in an increasingly ugly war of words with Russia over Ukraine, could be more than happy to oblige, provided that FIFA decides to hold a snap election on new bids. What soccer-mad nation, after all, wouldn't jump at the chance to host the World Cup?

And Russia is significantly concerned enough about its World Cup 2018 bid that both Vladimir Putin and the Russian Foreign Ministry have come out strong in defense of the World Cup bidding process, and most importantly, Russia's right to host the World Cup. Both the Kremlin and the Russian Foreign Ministry have questioned the U.S. jurisdiction in this matter, especially since none of the FIFA officials implicated were U.S. citizens. In an official statement, the Russian Foreign Ministry even called the FIFA arrests "illegal." Vladimir Putin suggested the U.S. was meddling in international affairs.

Who knows? Maybe the true reason for John Kerry's surprise visit to Sochi in May 2015 was to politely warn the Russians: "Ok, you pulled the wool over our eyes on Crimea. But there's going to be hell to pay for it."

The bad news for Russia is that it can't expect the FIFA World Cup scandal to be the last effort by the West to strip away the 2018 World Cup. In the following weeks, there were various negative articles in the media that could impact Russia's ability to host the World Cup, including the provocative story that Russia is conscripting prison labor to build everything needed for the World Cup as a way to keep costs down.

Yes, there's the old, recycled argument from the Sochi Olympics — the whole "this thing is going to be way too expensive" argument. And, of course, there's going to be the outcry over hosting World Cup events in places like Volgograd and Sochi (too close to the terrorism-prone Caucasus), and quite possibly, in any Russian cities located close to European hostilities over Ukraine (Kaliningrad, perhaps?).

Of course, maybe it's still too early to chalk all this up to a giant conspiracy to weaken and humiliate Russia. After all, Russia seems to see a conspiracy any time something bad happens to it in the world. If oil prices drop, it must be a vast U.S.-Saudi conspiracy, right? If violence breaks out in Europe, it must be some sinister plan to disrupt Russia's gas pipelines, right?

The best — and possibly, only — recourse for Russia right now is spin this FIFA corruption scandal as a Western effort to cripple the development of an emerging multipolar world. That's because the other World Cup bid that's under question is the 2022 Qatar bid. That means you have the West — led by the U.S. — ganging up on Russia AND the Middle East. That changes the narrative significantly.

You can already glimpse the broad outlines of such an approach from the Russian Foreign Ministry, which basically called the U.S. involvement in bringing to light the FIFA scandal an extraterritorial abuse of legal power: "Stop trying to hold court far beyond your own borders using your own legal norms." The reason this approach works is because it helps to focus the rest of the world on the times when the U.S. has used raw, naked power (both political and economic) under the guise of "international law" to achieve its goals.

From a purely geopolitical perspective, the West will have a lot harder time blocking the World Cup than the Winter Olympics. Forget the timing and complexity issues involved in taking away the Russian bid and handing it to someone else. It's simple logic — most of the nations competing on the skating rinks and the ice rinks in the Winter Olympics are European or North American nations. You don't see gold medal winners from Latin America, Africa or the Middle East on the podium.

But all that changes for the World Cup, where the BRIC nations and all the nations of sub-Saharan Africa and Latin America and Southeast Asia suddenly play a much larger role. If Russia can present itself as the true champion of a multi-polar world — and not as some lawless Russian bear running amok on the European continent — there may be hope that Russia can hold on to its World Cup 2018 bid and actually turn it into a useful extension of Russian soft power in the developing world.

Nothing is true and everything is possible with Russian propaganda

If there's any doubt that a sophisticated "information war" exists between Russia and the West, look no further than how the 2014 book by self-proclaimed "Russian TV insider" Peter Pomerantsev has exploded into the Western mainstream media.

Before the annexation of Crimea in March 2014, "Nothing is True and Everything is Possible" would have been shrugged off as just another in the long line of "you won't believe how surreal Moscow is" tales told by a Western expat. However, given the current geopolitical tensions between Russia and the West, Pomerantsev's book has been transformed into the definitive study of Russian TV propaganda at work and yet more evidence of the morally dubious Russian political culture created by the Kremlin.

But something's wrong here.

Ellen Mickiewicz, an expert on Russian media and a professor of political science at Duke University, has pointed out on her Facebook page that there is actually very little in the book that qualifies as an "insider account"—Pomerantsev himself was simply a junior Western expat in Moscow during the 2000s who was trying to sell "junk" reality TV shows to TNT (their TNT, not our TNT). In the book, Pomerantsev even admits that Western expats were closed off from the inner sanctum where key decisions are made, leaving them as outsiders.

The one scene that everyone's talking about as the result of a prominent February 13 profile in the *New York Times*—the one where Pomerantsev is the most junior person at a meeting in a conference room at the top of the Ostankino Tower in Moscow and producers are talking about how to script the weekly news for a credulous Russian TV audience — is from nearly a decade ago:

"In 2001, at age 24, he goes to visit Moscow and works on junk shows: soap operas, gangsters, and what the *New York Times* calls "sinister cults." He says he was "at a meeting" with a "prominent news anchor" who actually, yes actually, reviewed upcoming issues and "mused on how best to entertain the audience and questioned who that week's enemy should be." That a newspaper—national and international, of great stature and history could devote more than half a page to this naive "OH, MY GOODNESS!!" REVELATION is unbelievable. And it gets worse: thanks to "slick" new TV techniques the Kremlin has the world at its feet—no longer the boring Soviet TV."

As a result, in "Nothing is True and Everything is Possible," we get what you would expect from a young twenty-something finding himself in Russia still in the middle of radical transformation: a fast-paced narrative in which Russian society appears to be rapidly falling apart at the seams. As a young reality show TV producer in Moscow, Pomerantsev was there to lap it up — the impossibly beautiful Russian women who take courses on how to become gold-diggers, the mafia toughs from the Siberian provinces who learned how to act like mafia dons by watching "The Godfather," the self-made multimillionaire bankers literally throwing money around the streets of Moscow, the seedy underworld of mystical cults and Hell's Angels-like biker gangs.

And yet, these are exactly the types of stories you might expect to see on an American reality show segment on any given night in America. The show Pomerantsev seems to be most proud of—the Russian version of "How to Marry a Millionaire"—is a good example. It was a show he produced. Those Russian gold-diggers he describes could be the Kardashians cavorting around Los Angeles, those impossibly blond and perky girls working at Ostankino could be the blonde anchor girls of CNN and Fox News, and the bizarre characters appearing on reality shows from across the vast expanse of Russia could be the bizarre characters on America's never-ending virtual reality shows such as "The Real Housewives" or "Duck Dynasty."

So what's the big reveal?

The crux of the book—and the reason why it is being promoted so heavily in Western media circles—is that a chance meeting in Ostankino shows the rot at the heart of Russia's "scripted reality." (Putin appears in the book, but only as "the President," presumably to make it past Western, not Russian, censors.)

Everything takes on sinister tones. The gleaming Ostankino tower becomes the "nerve center of the Russian media machine." Russian TV becomes a strange form of "Soviet control with Western entertainment." Russia becomes a "vast scripted reality show" with a "puppet opposition," cartoon-like businessmen, and a citizenry on the brink of becoming unwitting victims of mystical soothsayers and fast-buck scam artists.

Where the new book fits into the current information war with West is clear—it's part of a broader effort by the Western media elite to paint modern Russia as a morally bankrupt nation, as a rogue state outside of the Western value system. In the West, the information war is not be waged on TV, as in Russia, but on the op-ed and culture pages of America's best newspapers.

The review of the book that appeared in the *New York Times* on November 30, 2014 was written by Miriam Elder, who has turned BuzzFeed into a buzz saw against Russia. The review of the book in the *Wall Street Journal* on December 8 was written by Karen Dawisha, who has written her own book about Putin's Russia called "Putin's Kleptocracy." The same weekend that a sweetheart Valentine's Day profile of Pomerantsev appeared in the *New York Times*, there was also a rave review in the *Washington Post*.

More importantly, Pomerantsev—who freely admits he was a junior producer always on the lookout for new scripts to sell while in Moscow (and even back home in London)—has parlayed his writing for a number of elite Western media outlets and critical success of the book into a think tank tour featuring a report ("The Menace of Unreality") on "how the Kremlin weaponizes information," financed in part by Kremlin critic Mikhail Khodorkovsky. (Not directly, of course, but the way the Russians do it—through a "shell organization" known as The Institute of Modern Russia.) In the increasingly crowded American media landscape, apparently, the only way to stand out now is to pitch your book like a reality TV show and then find a wealthy donor to support it.

Which is not to say that the book does not have its merits. Did I mention that it has lurid details of "suicidal supermodels," "oligarch revolutionaries," "professional killers," and "Hell's Angels as Holy Warriors"? There's a fascinating sketch of Russian "puppet-master" Vladislav Surkov. It reads convincingly—until you check out the endnotes and realize that the entire chapter of the book on Surkov has been cobbled together from news accounts and a brilliant article by Zoya Svetova ("Who is Mr. Surkov?"). If you haven't been in Moscow lately, you will also learn some nice bits of Russian slang—a "Forbes" is apparently the term of the moment for what Americans for years have called a "Sugar Daddy."

Take a step back, and you realize that the reason why the West and Russia are now headed on a geopolitical collision course is not because they have moved further apart on the ideological spectrum, but because they have moved so close together. Russia is the "nouveau riche" geopolitical upstart trying to take over from the "old money" West, and as a result, there's a lot of sniffing and huffing about a bunch of Russian multimillionaires throwing their money around and acting so crassly.

Russians, the Western media elite gatekeepers say, are "co-opting" the West, borrowing all of our terms and expressions and using them in dubious new ways. That is actually a key insight from Pomerantsev that emerges from his narrative almost accidentally. Westerners came to Russia in the political vacuum created by the collapse of Communism and the failed policies of Yeltsin's gangster oligarchy and flooded it with all the perks and goodies of Western society: the high-priced MBA consultants selling democratization projects, the new business models, the political technologists, the democracy specialists, the elusive goal of a civil society and the fetishization of luxury consumer products.

In Russia, after "faking it" for so long under Communism, it's now easy to simulate just about anything—including the trappings of Western democracy. And that's why the current Russian media world almost seems to be mocking the West with its "pretend Western society." According to Pomerantsev, there's a media exec at RT who dresses up like an Edwardian-era dandy, speaks brilliant English, and invites Brits for a nice round of golf—in snowy Moscow! (Pomerantsev says he must be an FSB spy.) There's also Julian Assange and Larry King hosting shows on RT. (Larry King!)

That's what scares Pomerantsev. Russia is co-opting everything the West has ever created and turning it inside out. That's never more accurate than when he's describing Russia's "Golden Youth" at play in London. As Pomerantsev points out, "The Kremlin has been co-opting the West for years."

But isn't that what the West wanted all along from Russia—a "pretend" Western society that looked and acted just like the West, only filled with gleaming onion domes and white, fluffy snow? The West wanted a pliant Russian society filled with new consumers—not just of its products, but also of its culture and ideology. That's what all the Western NGOs preached to Russia in the 1990s and 2000s—democratization and privatization. So whose fault was it that "privatization of business" was soon misinterpreted by Surkov to mean the "privatization of politics"?

No doubt, there is a new visual aesthetic emerging in Russia made possible by state-run TV, in which the strange mélange of Orthodox figures, revolutionary oligarchs in exile abroad, and slick gangsters all play a part. But is that really any different from the cartoon-like political figures that have emerged in America? Watch the Sunday news talk shows on American cable TV. You couldn't make up someone like Sarah Palin. Americans, just like modern Russians, "laugh and ignore the propaganda and watch the good stuff."

As a thought experiment, imagine a particularly clever Russian working in New York City media and advertising circles for a decade and coming back to Moscow with wonderful zingers about the "liars" at NBC (sorry, Brian Williams), the buffoonish political characters that populate our political universe (sorry, Donald Trump), the junk programming on cable TV that placates America's consumer masses. If Russian political life is scripted, what exactly should the Russians think of the potential for another Bush-Clinton presidential campaign race in 2016? When it's 3 Bush family members rotating in and out of the presidency, it's OK (wink, wink), but when it's Vladimir Putin 3 times in a row, there's something fishy going on.

If you're looking for insights into how the Russian elites use modern media, you're better off reading one of Ellen Mickiewicz's books. As a fast and loose account of Moscow during the oil boom years, Pomerantsev's book is a fun and entertaining read. When it tries to show Russia as being a surreal sham society, though, the book turns into an uncomfortable mirror of what Western society has become, in which democracy and freedom have become buzzwords that America's politicians throw around the world indiscriminately and apply as they see fit.

Viewed from that perspective, Mickiewicz asks a valuable question about how the *New York Times* opted to promote its profile of Pomerantsev: "Does the headline 'Russian TV Insider Describes a Modern Propaganda Machine' make any sense at all?"

Putin's new Crimea documentary is the ultimate scripted reality

Which is not to say that Russia has not played a role in the "information war" with the West. State-run media in Russia is all too willing to craft specific messages for domestic consumption.

The 2015 Russian-language documentary film about Crimea ("Crimea: The Way Home") is a slick piece of filmmaking— combining historical footage from events over the past year in Ukraine, historical re-enactments of key scenes that led to Russia re-taking Crimea one year ago, interviews with top Crimean officials and local heroes, and most importantly, an extended interview with Russian President Vladimir Putin.

But the documentary is an even slicker piece of Russian "scripted reality," combining all the greatest hits of Russia's propaganda about Ukraine over a period of two and one-half hours, told in an entertaining and compelling way. Suffice it to say that there are scenes of crazed Ukrainian nationalists burning buses and plenty of references to the West instigating a coup in Kiev with specific language and sentiment that hews closely to the Kremlin line on what went down in Crimea.

The trailer for Putin's new Crimea documentary, released just days before the premiere on Russian TV on March 15, 2015 had already produced a bombshell effect in Western capitals, in the form of Putin "confessing" in an interview clip with Andrey Kondrashov that the decision to annex Crimea had been taken on the night of February 22, 2014 well before the March 16, 2014 referendum that resulted in Crimea being returned to Russia.

There are at least five other elements in "Crimea: The Way Home" that are almost certain to piss off diplomats in Washington and Brussels - or at least former U.S. State Department spokeswoman Jen Psaki, who became a favorite target of Russian state-run media for her flimsy explanations of U.S. actions abroad.

First and most importantly, it now appears that Russia is never giving Crimea back, ever. Let's start with the title: "Crimea: The Way Home." In a literal translation of the Russian title, it's more precisely translated as "Crimea: The Path Back to the Motherland." This implies that Crimea has been—and always will be—part of Russia. It's not so much Russia wresting away something that has never belonged to it, but merely reclaiming possession over the peninsula. Bottom line for the West: Russia is never, ever giving Crimea back.

The film also positions the "Crimean Spring" as a reaction to the coup in Kiev. That settles the matter of how to describe what exactly went down in Crimea in February and March 2014. Was it an "annexation," an "incorporation," an "accession," or a "unification"? Well, this new documentary has the answer—all the events took place as part of the "Crimean Spring," so that means it must have been a "unification."

In such a way, the documentary positions the events in Crimea in the same way as the "Arab Spring" events in the Middle East or— as the natural uprising of people against their unlawful and unscrupulous masters. It was not an "act of aggression" by an external state—it was the voice of the people being expressed in a great uprising of democracy.

The film also makes clear that Russia is willing and able to use the nuclear option. Maybe it's all a bit of bluster, but Vladimir Putin tells Kondrashov in the documentary that Russia was willing to use the "nuclear option" to protect Crimea. At some point, he was willing to put Russia's strategic nuclear forces on high alert if it meant protecting Russian interests in Crimea. So it's perhaps no surprise that Russia is now blustering about returning nukes to Crimea. Because, well, nobody messes with a nuclear-armed peninsula.

In the film, Putin cements his role as the ultimate unreliable narrator for the West. How about the fact that Vladimir Putin claims that he was personally orchestrating the events in Crimea, including the evacuation of deposed Ukrainian leader Yanukovych? Putin said that he had personal radio contact with the team leading Yanukovych's evacuation, and was personally overseeing the deployment of the "little green men" in Crimea. This is going to play big at home, where Russians want a strong leader.

In the West, perhaps the closest example of a top leader personally overseeing such a high-profile operation is when Obama and members of his team (including Hillary Clinton) were personally watching the takedown of Osama Bin Laden via a live video feed.

But consider this — the whole documentary is basically Russian President Vladimir Putin narrating what happened in February and March 2014. Sure, there is airtime given to Russian Defense Minister Shoigu and all the local Crimean heroes, but the narrative is completely driven by Putin. He's narrating history, telling the West exactly how he did it.

And, yet, Russian propaganda's scripted reality is actually entertaining. "Crimea: The Way Home" has the feel of a History Channel documentary, with historical reenactments spliced together with brief interviews with key supporting players to give depth to the extended Putin commentary. It's a strange mix of theatricality, melodrama and nationalism. You do get the impression that just about everyone in Crimea wanted this to happen.

There's also the appearance of Russian propaganda's stock characters—hard-working Crimean Tatars eager to rejoin Russia, members of the nationalist motorcycle group "Night Wolves," everyday Crimeans trudging off to battle evil usurpers from Kiev with their riot shields painted a patriotic red, white and blue for Russia and the appearance of the very lovely Crimean public prosecutor Natalia Poklonskaya (who sits down for tea with Kondrashov on a hill overlooking the Black Sea near the end of the documentary). There's even a Crimean blacksmith who's working in some kind of underground forge to make all those aluminum riot shields for the heroic people of Ukraine.

For Kremlin critics such as Peter Pomerantsev (author of "Nothing is True and Everything is Possible") concerned that Russian propaganda already is a form of "scripted reality"—this is going to be yet more proof that Russia is bringing some pretty slick TV production values to its propaganda efforts.

Crimea, they'll say, is just one big scripted reality show for the Kremlin. Consider that partial interviews were conducted in a charred-out bus. Another interview takes place on a desolate-looking dried-up seabed (blamed on Kiev, of course). The documentary ends, of course, with the sun rising over the Black Sea and a triumphant note of hope.

Throughout the documentary, Putin takes special pains to point out that Russian troops were used sparingly as part of a defensive military operation—and that leaves NATO looking very bad by way of comparison. How did they not see this coming? No wonder NATO is spooked now that a similar type of operation involving "little green men" (Russia prefers to call them "polite people") could happen just about anywhere in Europe.

With this new Crimea documentary, Russia is essentially writing history and disseminating its version of the events around the world. Already there are plans to distribute Putin's new Crimean documentary in other languages.

During the live airing of the program on Russian TV in March 2015, commercial advertisements were basically limited to previews of new historic film projects coming up, including one on the "hero city" of Sevastopol in Crimea.

History, as they say, belongs to the victors, and Russia is basically telling the West: "We won, and we're going to tell you exactly what happened." In the age of YouTube and the rise of the Internet as a rich visual medium, Russian TV is turning out be a remarkably powerful tool. In just the first 48 hours after the documentary aired, there were over 2 million views on YouTube. In this "information war," it's clicks and views that matter and the easiest way to keep track of who's winning and who's losing.

Geopolitical Conspiracies

"Russia is a riddle, wrapped in a mystery, inside an enigma."

- Winston Churchill (1939)

The West has run out of ways to talk about Russia

It seems like Winston Churchill was right when he famously suggested that Russia was "a riddle, wrapped in a mystery, inside an enigma." Nowhere is that more evident than in what is happening right now in Ukraine. The West simply can't figure out what's going on with Russia and why the Kremlin acted so forcefully to annex Crimea and then support the separatists of Donetsk and Luhansk.

Angela Stent, director of the Center for Eurasian, Russian and East European Studies at Georgetown University, has weighed in on the op-ed pages of the *Washington Post* with her own take on "Why America Doesn't Understand Russia." Stent points to the disturbing trend of viewing the study of Russia as simply a passing "academic fad" rather than as a comprehensive scholarly discipline that involves an understanding of the region and its languages, history, culture, economy and politics.

"Unfortunately, America's focus on Russia comes and goes with news cycles and academic fads. Over the past decade or so, growing interest in China and the Arab world sidelined Russia; at most, it was one-fourth of the BRIC acronym of emerging markets — and the least enticing," writes Stent. "But now, the trifecta of Edward Snowden, the Sochi Olympics, and the Ukraine crisis has prompted talk of a new Cold War and how hard Vladimir Putin will play 'great power' politics..."

Stent continues: "Sovietology may be as defunct as the Soviet Union itself. But the need for a dedicated and deep understanding of Russia — especially the motives and machinations emanating from the Kremlin — is as critical as ever. Otherwise the United States is doomed to repeat cycles of "resets," great expectations of better relations with Russia followed by serial disappointments. President Obama's reset was only the latest of four since the Cold War ended."

Ms. Stent makes a great point — if we don't put serious money, time and attention into educating the next generation of Russian scholars, then America will end up repeatedly flat-footed anytime Russia makes a move in the world. We won't know what's happening now so we will turn to the past for explanations.

In the months after escalating tension on the Crimean peninsula, the West's best Russia experts reached deep into Russian history to develop a suitable framework for understanding the latest steps by Russia and its (seemingly inscrutable) president, Vladimir Putin. As of yet, nobody has provided a satisfying answer. (Even Germany's Angela Merkel, herself a fluent Russian speaker, has apparently already given up.) The Kremlin, as always, remains a black box.

Just consider some of the theories being tossed around by today's Russia experts. The core theory, of course, is that this is the Cold War, redux. Given that the Cold War between the U.S. and Russia is still fresh in everyone's memory, it's no surprise that various versions of "Cold War II" are making the rounds.

Considering that the Soviet Union just broke part in the early 1990s, just about everyone over the age of 35 in the U.S. — not just older Baby Boomers and senior members of Congress — has probably grown up with some kind of misconception about Russia as a result of the Cold War era.

Some misperceptions are more deeply ingrained than others. No wonder that most people think we're headed for Cold War II as a result of Crimea. If the U.S. has nukes, and Russia has nukes, and we're still squabbling over geopolitics in places like Ukraine, it makes sense to trot out all the Cold War tropes, right?

Wrong.

The problem is that all this misplaced talk of "Cold War II" has led to the latest round of Red baiting in the media and McCarthyism-style witch hunts against pro-Russia Russian scholars in the media. It's now fashionable to proclaim any pro-Russian intellectual in America as a "dupe" or a "stooge" of Putin, just as all left-leaning intellectuals were "dupes" and "stooges" of Communism and Joseph Stalin.

The one public intellectual who has taken the most heat for his views, of course, is Stephen F. Cohen of Princeton University. Even daring to suggest that Putin's motives may be grounded in reason and rationality — that perhaps the West over-stretched a bit when it extended NATO to the very borders of Russia — is met with a round of furious denunciations in the media.

But Russia experts have gone back even a few more decades in their quixotic quest to understand Russia's motivations. If you're Hillary Clinton, then the clearest example, of course, has to be Hitler and the Sudetenland. This pseudo-explanation (Putin = Hitler) tends to resonate far and wide in American media circles, especially given the historical parallels, like

Germany's hosting of the 1936 Summer Olympics and Hitler's moves to annex part of Europe.

For people looking for a quick and easy explanation, Putin is Hitler, Sochi is Berlin, and the Crimea is Sudetenland. Problem solved. If you buy into these mental model of Russia, then it's relatively easy to crank out a magazine cover these days — just depict Putin as a 21st century Hitler.

Of course, resorting to Nazi Germany parallels is a bit too intellectually dishonest and controversial these days (especially if you're planning on running for the U.S. Presidency in 2016), so the best Russian scholars are busy looking for new parallels in Russia's past. Maybe it all has to do with a perceived slight that Russia received during the post-Cold War period? Maybe there's something to be mined from the Brezhnev era? Maybe there's something to be learned from the Yeltsin or Gorbachev era?

If you want to make your mark as a Russian expert, though, there's no point in stopping the Wayback Machine in 1991. Let's crank it to 11 and go all the way back to the Stalinist era! Let's go back to the 1850s and the original battle for Crimea! Let's go back to the era of Boris Godunov and the Time of Troubles! Let's invoke Russia's most famous tsars, from Ivan the Terrible to Catherine the Great, for an explanation for Putin's motives. Let's blame it all on the Mongol invaders, who repeatedly burned down Moscow and turned Russia into a deeply troubled adolescent nation that failed to undergo a Renaissance or Enlightenment. Let's turn the clock back to Kievan Rus and mull over all the myths and identity problems plaguing Russia today as a result of events that happened almost a millennium ago.

You can see where the problem with this is — we've stopped learning about the modern Russia, and we've been reduced to analyzing Russia's actions from behind the safety of a desk and computer monitor. We're reading dusty old books about Russia instead of going out in the "Russian street" to find out the truth. In short, we've become lazy.

This, too, is a point that Angela Stent makes in her *Washington Post* column. Back in the day, she writes, it was OK to sit at your desk at an august academic institution like Harvard and attempt to divine the mysterious ways of the Soviet Union without having to do too much fieldwork. That's all changed since the breakup of the Soviet Union. Stent makes this clear:

"My doctoral adviser at Harvard, Adam Ulam, was a brilliant student of Soviet foreign policy, but he did most of his research sitting in his Cambridge office, trying to get inside the heads of Kremlin decision-makers. When I was in Moscow during the Chernobyl nuclear accident of 1986, a Western broadcast reporter called me to ask, "What does the man on the street in Moscow think?"

Stent continues: The answer was that the "man on the street" did not exist, at least in Western terms. He had not been told about the accident and would not have dared talk to a random American asking questions on that street, anyway. [...] But today, it is possible to meet for hours with Putin, as I have done every year over the past decade, and challenge him with questions. And it is possible to learn what a wide variety of

Russian men and women think—both on the street and in the square."

You can see where all this is headed. If we continue to devalue the importance of Russian area studies and resort to deeply unsatisfying theories of Russia based on what's happened in the distant past, we'll eventually end up turning to Hollywood or late night television for our insights about Russian foreign policy. We'll actually believe that Liam Neeson of "Taken" holds the secret to dealing with President Putin, or that ridiculously complex foreign policy problems can be solved with the ease and aplomb of a Stephen Colbert one-liner. With the Internet, of course, any of these simplistic views of Russia can be relentlessly distributed to the masses with a few funny photos, a brief video clip on YouTube, a clever hashtag, and an outrageous title.

It doesn't have to be this way, but it will require some tough choices in academia. Russian studies shouldn't be a fad or a field of endeavor that vanishes when Russian news vanishes from the headlines. As Ms. Stent suggests, "Unless we commit to educating a new generation about this onetime rival and possible partner, we won't be prepared to deal effectively with Russia's post-Putin generation, with all the risks and challenges—but also the opportunities—it will present."

America's paranoid war game fantasies about Putin's Russia

In many ways, the information war between Russia and the West has already influenced the way Western analysts view all of Russia's foreign policy moves. Now inclined to view Russia as an aggressor state, these analysts are filled with growing concern that the "hybrid war" in Ukraine could widen to greater Europe.

A map of Europe, appearing in the March/April 2015 issue of *Modern War* magazine (a publisher of military strategy games), purported to show "Putin's vision of Europe for 2015." Based on the compiled speeches, papers and offhand remarks of Russian President Vladimir Putin and his advisers, it's the ultimate war gamer fantasy of how dangerous an aggressive an expansionist and imperialist Russian might become for Europe.

On the map, parts of Ukraine have been lopped off to create Donbas, Crimea and Novorossiya ("New Russia"). The Baltic States have been partitioned to make room for ethnic Russian states in Narva and Dvinsk. Transnistria appears as a separate nation-state. Georgia has been partitioned into Western Georgia and Kakheti, bookended on either side by "Russian Abkhazia" and the "Caucasus Emirates." To make that possible, there's a "heavily-patrolled autobahn-type highway" giving Russia a narrow corridor of access to the South Caucasus.

And consider all the other audacious changes on this map of Europe—Germany appears to have expanded significantly both eastward and westward; there's a new "ghetto-like mini-state" called "Arab Piedmont" for Western Europe's restive Muslim population; and England and Spain have been partitioned due to separatist movements in Scotland and Catalonia, respectively. Turkey has carved out part of Bulgaria to form "Turkish Burgas." (Perhaps as compensation for partnering with Russia on a huge new gas deal?) Eastern Europe has become a mess of small states — Chelm, Galicia, Carpathian Rus, Bukovina and Bessarabia.

According to Gilberto Villahermosa, the author of the "Putin as Warlord" piece that accompanies the map in *Modern War* magazine, "The resurgence of Germany to its prewar 1939 borders in the east, and those of 1914 in the west, would be engineered as payoff to Berlin for letting all the other changes take place." It's another Molotov-Ribbentrop Pact, this time engineered between Putin and Merkel! And we thought they didn't like each other!

Despite the war gamer fantasy component of a new Russian-German conspiracy to divide up Europe, the contours of this map may not be as crazy as they first appear. Russia continues to play its political and energy sector cards, playing off one European state against another in search of strategic advantage. And there is a historical precedent for many of these moves. Back in September 2014, Robert Coalson wrote in *The Atlantic* of how legendary dissident Alexander Solzhenitsyn in 1990 predicted many of the moves Putin is making today in the post-Soviet space. Last June, Frank Jacobs used an eerily similar type of scenario in *Foreign Policy* explaining "What Russia Could Look Like in 2035, if Putin Gets His Wish."

That being said, the "Putin as Warlord" thesis trades too much on war gamer fantasies. In the piece, there's extended analysis of

Russia's need for steel and wheat, of the imperative to boost population in order to field bigger and better armies. Putin is described as a modern-day warlord who is using Russian military power to restore Russian greatness, the same way that Hitler used German military power to bring back German greatness. And, to top it all off, there's a hilarious Photoshopped image of Putin as an aging Brezhnev-type figure in Soviet military regalia. Because there's nothing scarier than the return of the once mighty USSR.

The weird way that ISIS is changing the way we talk about Russia

Something has perceptibly changed in the way Western media covers Russia – the forecasts of what's happening within Russia are becoming more hysterical (just consider the media reaction to #WhereisPutin), the willingness to engage militarily is stronger, and the propaganda war is intensifying in scale and scope. You could chalk all this up to the escalation of the crisis in Ukraine, of course, but here's another idea: ISIS is changing the way we talk about Russia.

The "ISIS narrative," in short, is starting to shape the "Russia narrative." Watch CNN long enough, and you will get an intuitive feel for how this happens – a story on ISIS will immediately cut to a story about MH17 or the separatists in eastern Ukraine or the Boris Nemtsov murder. Even without realizing it, our brains may be programmed to process these events from two very different parts of the world in the same way – as just a giant nexus of terrorism, violence and masked men doing very bad things.

There's actually a scientific explanation for this. Nobel Prize-winning psychologist Daniel Kahneman, together with Amos Tversky, identified a specific type of cognitive bias known as the "availability heuristic." In the face of uncertainty, they say, the human brain instinctively searches for the most available information to help it make sense of an unfamiliar situation. The brain is hard-wired to believe that the information or theory that is most available is also what's most important. It's what makes people believe that shark attacks, homicides and being struck by lightning are so common – those stories are so available in the media that we believe they are significantly more likely to happen than they really are.

In the face of uncertain Russian actions, then, the Western media has become a victim of a specific form of this availability heuristic. Faced with an escalating crisis in Ukraine, the West has been biased by what's happening elsewhere in the Middle East. As Kahneman might say, instead of thinking slow, the West is thinking fast.

You could see the first signs of this in September 2014, when President Obama inexplicably mentioned Russia as the #2 threat to international peace and stability in his address to the UN in late September. The Russians, understandably, were baffled.

And that's been followed up with changing optics in the mainstream media that are starting to blur the ISIS narrative and the Russia narrative. This includes a bizarre piece in *The Daily Beast* ("Ukraine Rebels Thank Jesus for Victory") from the otherwise wonderfully talented Anna Nemtsova, who painted the Ukrainian separatists as some kind of Russian Orthodox jihadis intent on creating Novorossiya with the help of Jesus.

Or, consider a recent piece by Michael Cecire for *Foreign Policy* ("The Kremlin Pulls on Georgia"), which describes groups of pro-Russian operatives "protesting in Tbilisi Streets, preaching in Georgian churches." This is the same way the mainstream media describes the "Arab Street" and imams in mosques in stories about ISIS.

Yes, the more the media mentions ISIS militants, the Islamic caliphate and the clash of civilizations, the easier it becomes to talk about Russian "militants" (not "separatists" or "freedom fighters"), the restoration of the Soviet empire (which somehow blurs together with the establishment of an Islamic Caliphate) and the clash of values between Europe and Russia (which is starting to strangely mimic the clash of values between Christianity and Islam). That's a dangerous new development.

Consider the way that we now talk about the "clash of civilizations" between the West and Russia. While Russia has always historically veered between Europe and Asia, it has never closed itself off from the West. Russia is Europe and Europe is Russia. But the concern that ISIS is encouraging a clash of civilizations between Islam and the West is also encouraging the media to frame Russia's confrontation with the West in the same terms.

Look at the rhetoric coming from Europe's top thinkers. You have George Soros calling Russia an "existential threat" and you have British Foreign Secretary Philip Hammond calling Russia the "single greatest threat" to Britain (even bigger than the threat from ISIS). At the same time, you have BuzzFeed posting "destruction porn" photos from eastern Ukraine, so it's getting easier and easier to connect the dots between the destruction in Iraq or Syria and the destruction in Novorossiya. *This is a foreign civilization that will burn Western civilization to the ground*, the images seem to say.

That paranoia about a clash of civilizations is based, in no small part, to the rapid extension of ISIS into states across the Middle East. The desire to build a caliphate is deeply troubling, especially when the likes of Boko Haram and Al Qaeda are somehow linked as part of some kind of global terror brand. ISIS is seemingly everywhere, a marauding army that will establish a new empire.

That's making it easier to ascribe similar types of imperialistic ambitions to Russia. The same way that ISIS is carving up the Middle East, Russia must be seeking to carve up Europe, right? There is the tendency to see Russian imperialistic aims everywhere to reclaim the former Soviet Union as if it were some kind of Russian Orthodox caliphate. The Baltic States, Kiev, Eastern Europe, Georgia, Kazakhstan – they've all been part of rumors in recent weeks, concerned about signs of a Russian military buildup in the region.

All of this is leading to a massive ratcheting up of the global propaganda war. Every day, we're told how ISIS is using Facebook to recruit volunteers, how Twitter is being used by ISIS as part of some kind of cyberwar, of how social media is luring young Westerners to fight for ISIS.

That media attention on the evil impact of ISIS propaganda makes it easier to see a similar type of propaganda war at work between the Russia and the West. Instead of viewing the Russian position on Ukraine as just a different take on the issue – the equivalent of the Palestinians or Iranians offering their counter-take on a complex foreign policy matter – we see it as the hand of a sinister propaganda machine cranking out lies.

ISIS propaganda, Russian propaganda -- it all blurs together in the minds of American TV viewers. ISIS volunteers being recruited via social media start to sound a lot like Russian volunteers being recruited to fight in the Donbas.

At the end of the day, the willingness (whether intentional or not) to mix the narrative around ISIS and the narrative around Russia is dangerous. And it's not just the "availability heuristic" at work – there's also another cognitive bias at work – and that's the "availability cascade." In short, a complex idea starts to be described in very simple terms that are easy to be understood, and that makes it easier for it to "cascade" into the popular consciousness.

By simplifying Russian motivations, it's making it far too easy to condone military action in Ukraine, and it's making it harder and harder to find a diplomatic solution to the crisis. This is the new logic of hardliners in Washington: If this is indeed a "clash of civilizations," if indeed the Russians are intent on creating a new post-Soviet empire, then they must be stopped the way ISIS is stopped – with boots on the ground and lethal military hardware.

At one time, it looked like the ISIS threat might have encouraged Russia and the West to cooperate – now it looks like the ISIS threat might in some weird way lead the West to close the door on whatever slight diplomatic opening remained with Russia.

Boris Nemtsov vs. the Russian Leviathan

As long as Russia remains an enigma to the West, it's going to be extraordinarily difficult to shift the Western media narrative, which portrays Russia as an authoritarian state ruled by a ruthless kleptocrat. An event such as the brutal murder of opposition figure Boris Nemtsov in central Moscow in February 2015 would appear to fit this narrative perfectly.

That's because the gangland-style murder of Russian politician Boris Nemtsov in the center of Moscow — just steps away from the Kremlin and just 36 hours ahead of a major opposition march in the city — is not only appalling, it is also unfathomable to the Western psyche.

Perhaps the only way to understand such a provocative act is within the context of Andrey Zvyagintsev's Oscar-nominated film "Leviathan," which portrays the corruption, moral decay and raw power at the heart of modern Russia.

The film — a two-hour portrayal of a Leviathan state ruled by corruption, graft and absolute power — has been called "a political statement about the nature of contemporary Russia — about a terrifying Leviathan, a corrupt government without honor or conscience, where the Church protects the government and Christ has been essentially privatized by gangsters."

How else to explain how a murder in cold blood in late winter could have taken place in the center of Moscow?

One scene in "Leviathan" especially stands out. Having decided that the system no longer works — that the Russian legal system is just a façade to protect the power of the local authorities — a middle-aged Moscow lawyer (played by Vladimir Vdovichenkov) goes head-to-head with the mayor of a northern provincial city by resorting to the one threat that is universally understood everywhere in modern Russian: the threat of a more powerful sponsor, backed by the release of kompromat.

All of this takes place under the watchful gaze of a portrait of Vladimir Putin in the mayor's office. The point made by Zvyagintsev is chilling: "You may threaten me now with all of your laws and kompromat, but I am protected by a higher power."

"Leviathan" makes clear that raw power only respects raw power. Raw power believes that it is possible to take what is desired by any means possible and that it is allowable to preserve power at all costs. In the film, everyone's in on the action — the local militia, the police, the church, the courts and the mayor's office. The only way to break the power of this system is by threatening to release compromising materials that are devastating enough to force a realignment of the power structure. And, even if this proof exists, it only matters if you are able to prove that your sponsor is more powerful than your opponent's sponsor.

And, this, unfortunately, is what the current murder case of Boris Nemtsov may be all about — his purported plan to divulge secrets about the secret Russian military presence in Ukraine. This was the ultimate kompromat and for this, some say, he was murdered. One of the most recognizable young liberal reformers in Russia in the 1990s and now a leading Kremlin critic, Nemtsov is reminiscent of the Moscow lawyer in the movie trying to go head-to-head with the Leviathan. In life, as in the film, the ending is brutal, senseless violence that leaves everyone with an inescapable sense of hopelessness.

The only way this gangland murder of Nemtsov could have occurred is if some higher authority had given the signal that this was allowed, that this murder had been sanctioned. And that raises a whole host of uncomfortable scenarios. The highest authority in Russia, of course, is Russian President Vladimir Putin, and this appears to be the person that many — including former U.S. ambassador to Russia Michael McFaul — are pointing to when they say, "I cannot believe that they have killed my friend, Boris Nemtsov."

But there are plenty of other scenarios that are within the realm of possibility. It is almost impossible to believe that the order to murder Nemtsov came from the Kremlin. If they did not do this to Navalny, how could they do this to Nemtsov? "They" could be rogue Russian nationalists. "They" could be members of the opposition who ordered the murder to create a martyr. "They" could be external actors — either from Ukraine or the Caucasus — intent on destabilizing the Russian state.

A more likely scenario — described by Kremlin critic Mikhail Khodorkovsky just days before in a speech to the Chatham House think tank — is that there will soon be a winner-takes-all battle between rival clans in Moscow. In Russian terms, the "vertical of power" controlled by Putin is now facing a threat from another "vertical of power."

In Western terms, it is a "turf war," plain and simple. A murder steps away from the Kremlin is the equivalent of an upstart power attempting to show the Leviathan that he is more powerful. It is raw power vs. raw power, one "boss" against another "boss," just like in the American gangster movies. Either Putin finds and breaks the parties responsible for this heinous crime — or the forces arrayed against Putin may launch a more daring attack against the state, with the whole world watching. At the very least, it is a sign that the Russian elite has broken ranks.

As in the film "Leviathan," there will be a succession of steps before the final denouement, all of them cloaked in all the courtesies and slogans of the West, as both sides attempt to find out who is stronger. The call for "justice" in Moscow today — as in the film — is high-minded but the ending is more likely to be "vigilante justice" than any form of justice recognizable by leaders in Western capitals.

This is not a system that Putin created, but one that he inherited from the collapse of the Communist state, and that the Communist state inherited from the Tsarist state. *If you do not show that you are strong, people will think you are weak*. This has always been the inexorable logic that has guided Russia. If this is indeed a struggle between the Russian elite and the Russian opposition, or between different clans of the Russian elite, then we are all in trouble.

A lone Chechen gunman on the Kremlin's grassy knoll

The tragic murder of Boris Nemtsov in Moscow has already engendered many conspiracy theories, some of them worthy of the most wildly speculative conspiracy theories that surrounded the death of JFK.

The growing consensus that a group of radical Islamists killed Boris Nemtsov on Feb. 27, 2015 as some kind of revenge for his comments about *Charlie Hebdo*—a story now playing all over state-run Russian TV—is in many ways the most perfectly imperfect ending to a puzzling murder case that has fascinated the Russian media.

By following the "Caucasian Trail" (a term instantly recognizable to anyone in Russia) to Chechnya, arresting 5 suspects, and securing a confession of guilt from one suspect, the Kremlin gets to prove that it always gets its man. The head of Chechnya (Ramzan Kadyrov) gets another chance to show that he's loyal to Vladimir Putin and make some public announcements on Instagram (the Chechens have Instagram!) related to the suspect.

Russia-watchers in the West get to heave a collective sigh of relief that it was the Chechens behind this all, not the Russian government or some kind of rogue nationalist government-within-a-government. Finally, for the average Russian, the story of sinister Chechens from the North Caucasus committing a heinous revenge murder makes as much sense as anything else on state-run TV these days.

But there's so much that just doesn't add up in this version of the murder.

For one, you have a murder that took place in the very heart of one of the most policed and monitored areas in the world, and yet, none of the security cameras—including more than a handful attached to the walls of the Kremlin—that could have seen the murder take place actually saw it.

Secondly, no eyewitnesses actually saw the murder take place—the only eyewitness who could have possibly seen the murder—the beautiful 23-year-old Ukrainian model Anna Duritskaya who was with Nemtsov on the night of the murder— claims to have seen nothing. She didn't even stay around long enough for the funeral and she's now back in Kiev after being interrogated by investigators.

Thirdly, the security patrol in the area around the Kremlin apparently had the night off, so the security operatives who might have been following Nemtsov in the hours leading up to a huge protest march in Moscow were nowhere to be found. A mysterious car seen on the bridge belonged to the security services, but was being used as a freelance taxi on the night of the murder.

Fourthly, the Moscow police didn't arrive for 11 minutes until after the murder on the bridge. Again, in one of the most heavily patrolled and monitored places in the world.

Fifthly, the one piece of CCTV video footage that might have explained what actually took place is so grainy that it's hard to make out anything truly concrete. And a snow removal truck that appears to have played a role in the murder-conspiracy conveniently blocked the site of the murder when the shots rang out.

In other words, nobody really knows what took place, and even after the arrest of five suspects and a confession of guilt, the details are still sketchy. There's even a plot line involving the Russian security services in Grozny, where one Chechen suspect apparently blew himself up with a grenade. So maybe there were six people involved.

Six is a conspiracy.

So, let's think like conspiracy experts. Assuming that the Chechens were actually involved, there's the outside possibility that these guys were basically just "patsies" for someone higher up the political food chain. Using the JFK analogy, was Zaur Dadayev (the Chechen Lee Harvey Oswald) a lone gunman acting alone, or was he a "patsy" for an ultra-nationalist group, for someone within the Russian government, or even for the West?

This is not as crazy as it sounds. There's a whole history of the "Caucasian Trail" appearing again and again anytime there's a controversial criminal case in Russia. One classic example is the 2006 murder of Russian journalist Anna Politkovskaya on Putin's birthday, which was eventually blamed on a group of 10 Chechens, while scandalous whispers suggested that Russian oligarch Boris Berezovsky might have been behind it. Make the right connections in conspiracy-land, and one could just as easily blame the murder of Nemtsov on a syndicate of Chechens, who were somehow financed by an oligarch such as Mikhail Khodorkovsky looking to destabilize Russia.

Chechens, as everyone now knows in Russia, make the best villains. And the latest crop of Chechen suspects in the murder of Boris Nemtsov—including suspected gunman Zaur Dadayev—

look like they are straight out of central casting. Even before President Vladimir Putin promised to "rub them out in the outhouse" when he launched the first Chechen War back in 1999, Chechens have been accused of just about everything in Russia— blowing up apartment buildings, running the mafia, blowing up subways, holding hostages, depraving the nation's youth with narcotics, and being Islamic militants.

And it's not just in Russia where Chechens are demonized. Consider that the Boston Marathon bombing trial in the United States involved bomber Dzhokhar Tsarnaev, who is—you guessed it—"of Chechen origin." The cold-blooded mafia killers who made the hit on Denzel Washington at the end of "Training Day"? Chechens. The shadowy "most wanted man" in Philip Seymour Hoffman's last film? Yes, he's half-Chechen. The evil bad guy in "The Equalizer"? A Chechen. There's even a cartoon villain who fights Batman known as "The Chechen." For Americans, Chechens are either cartoon villains or total badasses, and that makes the current version of events at least somewhat plausible.

What this "Nemtsov Affair" needs is a Zapruder film. Well, there is a Zapruder film, of sorts, a terribly grainy Russian CCV video of what went down on the night of Feb. 27. The only problem is that the exact moment when the murder took place is obscured by a mysterious snow removal "cleaning car" that may or may not have been involved. (Online, it's possible to read a fascinating version of how the snow removal "cleaning car" played the key role in the whole murder.)

If Oliver Stone ever wants to make a new film about Russia (and signs are, he does)—here's one idea: Make a film about an assassination of a high-level political figure revered in the West. Add in some shadowy characters from the underworld. Introduce a grainy film that may or may not show what actually happened. Pepper the film with conspiracy theories about the state security services. Make the suspect a "patsy" who may or may not have been backed by higher authorities. Introduce a radical story twist involving the Grassy Knoll. (In this case, not actually a Grassy Knoll as in Dealey Plaza, more like the cobblestone knoll of Red Square). That's not just the plot line for "JFK"—that could also be the plot line for the real-life murder of Boris Nemtsov.

Russian conspiracies and foreign policy black swans

2014 was an unexpected year for Russian foreign policy – a year no expert could have predicted. It wasn't just Russia's annexation of Crimea and the hybrid war in eastern Ukraine, it was the whole head-spinning relentless downward tumble of global oil prices that threatened to wreck the ruble and eviscerate Russia's economy from the inside out.

So why, then, were the Russian foreign policy forecasts for 2015 as equally dull as the ones heading into 2014?

Yes, heading into 2015, we knew that tensions between Russia and the U.S. were likely to remain high, that the situation in Ukraine probably wouldn't get resolved anytime soon, and that low oil prices would continue to put pressure on Russia's domestic economy. Those are not so much forecasts for the year ahead as just extrapolations of events already in motion.

And that's the problem with much Western analysis of Russia – it tends to see the machinations of the Russian state as part of a relatively easy-to-predict long-term trend rather than as a nuanced reaction to impossible-to-predict events ("Black Swans") occurring in the world. Hence, the annexation of Crimea is typically seen as part of a broader, long-term strategy to reclaim the former Soviet Union rather than a short-term, tactical reaction to what was perceived in Moscow as a coup d'état in Kiev.

In an attempt to show how much Russia watchers fail to take into account when analyzing the Kremlin, here are just some of the Black Swan foreign policy events that might – hypothetically speaking – turn U.S.-Russian relations upside down in 2015 or 2016.

Pressure on the Euro reshapes Moscow's relations with Europe

This one might happen sooner rather than later, with all the noise that Greece made about an exit from the Euro at the start of 2015. The so-called "Grexit" would have a huge impact on the Euro, no matter what the economists and diplomats in Germany might say. If you thought the collapse of Lehman Brothers in 2008 was big, wait until you have people worried about the collapse of the Eurozone.

One big beneficiary of any "Grexit" would, of course, be Moscow. EU members would have very little interest in punitive sanctions against Russia at a time when their own economies threaten to unravel. If Russia were able to throw an economic lifeline to Greece or convince other nations of Europe to make noise about an exit from the Euro, it would help to break any sense of cohesion within the EU and possibly threaten the whole system of Euro-Atlantic cooperation.

Instability in Saudi Arabia abruptly reverses the downward spiral in global oil prices

If you buy into the whole "Putinization of energy" thesis of Marin Katusa that he describes in his recent bestselling book "The Colder War," then it's clear that what happens in Saudi Arabia has huge implications for Russia. Saudi Arabia is the linchpin of the whole petrodollar system engineered by the U.S. in the mid-1970s and a long-time supporter of the U.S. While Saudi Arabia and

OPEC may not have the same sway as they once did 40 years ago, there's no denying that they still have the ability to influence global oil prices in a big way.

That's why any political instability within Saudi Arabia would be a huge windfall for Russia. That's because any instability within the country (either from contenders to the Saudi monarchy or from the Islamists) would almost certainly result in new leaders who are resentful of the West and favorably disposed to Russia.

And it would almost certainly result in greater instability throughout the Middle East (possibly even a shooting war between Saudi Arabia and Iran if radical Islamists take power in Riyadh). And, that's right – with so much instability, disruption and mayhem in the Middle East, the price of oil would almost certainly spike upward.

Russia finds an unexpected high-profile member for Eurasian integration

2015 was supposed to be the big debut year for the Eurasian Economic Union, but it's been tough going so far, with just Belarus and Kazakhstan as original launch members alongside Russia and no chance of Ukraine joining anytime soon. But Armenia just signed up at the end of 2014, as did Kyrgyzstan, and there are rumors Azerbaijan might join as well. But think really big – what if Turkey, Iran, India or Egypt decides to join the process of Eurasian integration in 2015?

If the Eurasian Union starts to get viewed as more than just a reconstitution of the Soviet Union, we might be talking about a 1-2 punch of the Eurasian Union and the Shanghai Cooperation

Organization (SCO) to challenge EU and NATO as an economic and military alternative for nations in the Middle East or Asia. Most importantly, a beefed-up Eurasian Union would give Russia a bigger bargaining chip to convince the nations of Central Asia to turn away from the alluring advances of China.

Russia pulls off the peace conference of the year

Heading into 2015, the talk in foreign policy circles was of a potential "Moscow I" peace conference to stabilize the situation in Syria. While the Kremlin obviously has a vested stake in Syria's Assad regime, it has given off some mixed signals that it's willing to take into account the interests of the Syrian opposition and play the role of the big-time peacemaker. Now, with the bombing campaign against ISIS in Syria, the need for a formal peace settlement is more important than ever.

Hosting a major Syrian peace conference in Moscow in 2016 would be a big step forward in burnishing Russia's foreign policy image – especially in the Middle East, where it needs as many partners as it can find. A peace conference might not win Vladimir Putin a Nobel Peace Prize, but it might just change a few minds in the Western political establishment.

Cyber war replaces information war as the new mode of U.S.-Russian confrontation

Throughout 2014, "information war" was one of the buzzwords of the confrontation between Russia and the West. It referred not just to overt propaganda on the part of Russia and the use of state-owned television as a new tool to control public opinion, but also all attempts to introduce the "fog of war" into what was going on in Ukraine. Both Russia and the West accused each other of manipulating the truth, and the battle for the moral higher ground often revolved around something like a YouTube video or a tweet.

Nobody's expecting a major military confrontation between Russia and the West over Ukraine – that would be too apocalyptic to even consider – but there's no denying that cyber warfare might be one way for both sides to chip away at each other while still providing enough cover for "plausible deniability." In 2014, there were already accounts of Russian hackers breaking into computer networks of NATO, and in 2015, these were followed up by accounts of Russian hackers breaking into the Pentagon's email. Given the accusations of cyber warfare being leveled against North Korea by the U.S., cyber warfare is becoming an increasingly likely prospect for the next round of asymmetric warfare.

Project Double Eagle goes into overdrive

According to Marin Katusa in "The Colder War," the de-dollarization of the world economy is one of the primary geo-economic goals of the Russian government. In Chapter 11 of his book ("Twilight of the Petrodollar"), Katusa calls de-dollarization "Vladimir Putin's grand strategy for waging the Colder War and unseating the dollar." Conspiracy theorists have a sexier name for it: Project Double Eagle.

Anything Moscow can do to weaken the dollar (such as by pricing oil in gold instead of dollars), then, is in Russia's interests. One place to continue this offensive against the dollar would have been at an event such as the 2015 BRICS Summit in Ufa. Russia and China have already started to make noise about settling energy trades in rubles and yuan, and last year, one of the big announcements at the BRICS Summit in Fortaleza was the creation of a New Development Bank based in Shanghai.

There have been other signs that Russia is trying to find alternatives to institutions like SWIFT, the Bank for International Settlements (BIS) and the IMF, so don't be surprised if Russia makes another splashy announcement with partners such as China or Iran that supports the push toward de-dollarization.

Russia makes a new pivot -- to Africa

Russia's pivot to Asia got all the headlines in 2014, culminating with the massive $400 billion gas deal signed between Russia and China. And the deals kept coming throughout the year, as Russia made every effort to prove to the West that it had other partners and other options. After doing major new deals in China and India, there's not much that Russia could do for encore this year. So where will the new Russian pivot be in the months ahead?

One candidate would be Africa, where Russia might seek to counter growing Chinese power on the continent, a place where China is now an economic juggernaut. In 2009, China passed the U.S. to become Africa's biggest trading partner. China now gets one-third of its oil from Africa, from places like Nigeria, Mozambique and Angola. Any oil being supplied to China by Africa is oil that's not being supplied by Russia – and that gives Russia a real incentive to get more involved in Africa's future economic development. Too much African oil making its way to China dilutes the value of any Sino-Russian partnership.

Ukraine massively defaults on all of its debts

The financial situation in Ukraine is not just beyond bleak, it's almost catastrophic. The country can't pay back $17 billion in IMF financing, it can't get the U.S. or any other international lender to go along with some kind of bailout scheme to the tune of another $15 billion to $20 billion, and it has almost lost all chance of mending economic fences with Russia.

A Ukrainian debt default would have serious knock-on political consequences within the nation, including the probable breakup of the coalition government in Kiev and more domestic political squabbling in Ukraine. In a worst case, you get an unwelcome replay of Euromaidan, starring a whole new cast of very unhappy characters and new debate about what to do about eastern Ukraine.

Russia widens its counter-terrorism initiative against ISIS beyond Syria

While there have been disturbing signs of potential ISIS involvement in recent terrorist activity in Chechnya and the North Caucasus, Russia had not taken many visible steps to combat ISIS extremism at its source before the bombing of ISIS positions in Syria began in October 2015. In other words, Russia had previously preferred to combat Islamist extremism on home soil by cracking down on known terrorist organizations in the North Caucasus.

However, any signal that ISIS was threatening to destabilize either Central Asia or the North Caucasus could force Moscow's hand, leading to an enlarged bombing campaign against ISIS. That could lead to a fluid situation in the Middle East, in which Russia turns to Iran – or even Israel and Saudi Arabia – for support.

MH17 turns out to be a "false flag" operation after all

In summer 2014, MH17 was the leading headline story for so long, and then, suddenly, all the news about MH17 went dark. Even after the black box for MH17 was recovered, there still has been no definitive proof that a Russian-made Buk missile took down the airliner.

While some of the Kremlin's theories for the shoot down of MH17 – like a Ukrainian missile intended for Putin's private plane – sound like they've been launched in an Internet chat room by conspiracy addicts with way too much time on their hands, it's still not outside the realm of possibility that 2015 turns up new evidence that Russia (or the Eastern Ukrainian separatists) had no role at all in the shoot down. And just imagine what would happen if the blame, instead, shifted to Ukraine or the West for the tragedy of MH17.

And that's just the start. It's possible to think of many other Black Swan events that would turn the U.S.-Russian relationship upside down. Any major military escalation within Ukraine – possibly as a result of the Ukraine Freedom Support Act passed by the U.S. Congress during the final days of 2014 that authorizes the U.S. to provide lethal military aid to Ukraine – would certainly qualify. As would any Russian intervention in the Baltic States or Moldova.

And, of course, there's the blackest of all Black Swans – regime change in Moscow, financed and encouraged by the West, that ends Vladimir Putin's 15 years in power. If there's one thing that really scares the Kremlin, it's this scenario of a "color revolution" leading to regime change. It's not for nothing that Vladimir Putin used his speech at the UN in September 2015 to warn about the risk of the "export of revolutions" and the tragic results of America's "democracy promotion" abroad.

Western paranoia about Russia's Arctic strategy

Another Black Swan foreign policy event that might change the structure of U.S.-Russian relations would be a military conflict in the Arctic, a region that Russia views as increasingly important to its long-term development.

To understand what Russia is up to in the Arctic, you will need to throw out your atlases and your Mercator projection maps of the world. You'll need to delete Google Maps and Apple Maps from your smartphone. Instead, what you'll need to do is pull out another Mercator map— the famous "Septentrionalium Terrarum descriptio" of 1595 - considered by cartographers to be the first-ever dedicated map of the Arctic.

Once you get used to viewing the world from the admittedly disorienting perspective of the North Pole, you'll notice that there are a few oddities here—the inscription that a band of female pygmies inhabit an outlying island of Norway, the vast whirlpool and rivers at the top of the world, or the black magnetic mountain at the North Pole.

However, you can immediately see at a glance how Russia views the Arctic. It's a zone neatly divided into four competing spheres of interest. With the melting of the polar ice caps, you've suddenly making it possible to run boats through the Northern Sea Route year-round, discover new mineral and hydrocarbon resources in the frozen Arctic and, yes, set up armed fortifications nearby. There are rivers here, not icecaps, and competing spheres of interest. In short, the Arctic is not some frozen wasteland populated by polar bears, it's a giant waterway full of strategic possibilities.

You can see at a glance at the map of 1595 that not only is Russia a hulking Eurasian landmass extending from Russia to Asia, but it's also potentially a huge Arctic superpower. Check out the breadth and expanse—it's almost like a Leviathan of the High North extending from Scandinavia to the Bering Strait. The only other countries that come close to Russia in size are Canada, Norway and Denmark (by virtue of its claim to Greenland). These four nations all dwarf the size of the U.S. Arctic landmass (i.e. Alaska).

And Russia has been by far the most aggressive nation in asserting its international rights. Once Russia figures out a way to circumvent sanctions and import the right drilling technology to exploit those resources, it's pretty clear what's going to happen next—the Russian oil & gas machine is going to march to the High North in search of new assets to exploit. Moreover, Russia is going to look for ways to steadily increase the size of its Exclusive Economic Zone (EEZ) in the Arctic.

And that means Russia is going to look for a way to protect those assets. While the U.S. has been busy sending off tourist boats to gape at the melting ice caps and take pictures of the polar bears, Russia has been busy drafting up a major new expansion of its military assets in the Arctic. In March 2015, as part of its 2015 Index of Military Strength, the U.S.-based Heritage Foundation outlined the number of installations that Russia has planned or is planning in the Arctic.

Frankly, it's stunning. There are armed fortifications extending along the entire Arctic frontier of Russia. There's an expanding Russian naval presence based near Murmansk. And there are plans to protect and fortify the Northern Sea Route.

If the U.S. plans to build a missile shield in Europe, it's easy to see how Russia might respond—by making things very dicey for the U.S. by basing bomber fleets across its Arctic assets, as some analysts have suggested.

You don't need the implied threat of ICBMs streaming their way across the European continent—you just need a way to send some nuclear-armed bombers over the North Pole to put a scare into Canada and the U.S.

Melting ice caps in the Arctic also have important implications for Russia's navy. If there's one thing that Russia doesn't want to happen, it's for its navy to be boxed in. You could argue that's one key reason why Crimea so important—it gives Russia the ability to project power across Mediterranean, instead of being boxed in within the Black Sea. Now, look at what happens if Russian icebreakers and ships are able to patrol the Arctic. Suddenly, you've got a way to control some pretty important shipping routes at the top of the world.

Back in the 1600s, inspired by this Mercator map, the possibilities for commerce and exploration were so intriguing that they set off centuries of explorers to find both a Northwest Passage and Northeast Passage through the Arctic. According to one historical anecdote, the Russian tsar Ivan the Terrible heard about European explorers making their way through Russia's Arctic territory and ordered the men brought straightaway to Moscow for a private audience with the imperial court. That led to new thinking about ways Russia might also explore and colonize the Arctic.

It will be interesting to see what happens next with Russia's plans for the Arctic, especially with a major new upgrade for Russia's Arctic naval presence announced in summer 2015. It's clear that, despite international protestations to the contrary, we are witnessing the militarization of the Arctic. And that militarization of the Arctic is being made possible by a melting polar ice cap that's making an esoteric map of the Arctic from more than 400 years ago suddenly relevant once again today.

What the West doesn't get about Russia's new Arctic mythology

The standard Western media narrative is that Russia's push into the Arctic is little more than a naked power grab -- a rush to militarize the Arctic and a misguided attempt to exploit the region's natural resources. In reality, the Arctic is part of a broader national idea of what Russia is, what Russia stands for, and what role Russia should play on the global stage.

Perhaps the best American analogy for the Arctic is that it is Russia's "Wild West" – a physical space as well as an intellectual concept that's capable of galvanizing an entire population around some specific sense of Russian "greatness" and Russian "identity." Andrei Kolesnikov of the Carnegie Moscow Center refers to this as an "Arctic Mythology" – and that's exactly what it is - a meta-narrative of events, symbols and goals that is part of a broader national identity for Russia.

Marlene Laruelle's book "Russia's Arctic Strategies and the Future of the Far North" has perhaps one of the most evocative descriptions of this "Arctic Mythology" as it applies to Russia's nationalists, Eurasianists and Communists:

"The dominant Russian view of the Arctic is one of a Russian national territory and not of an 'ethno-region.' This view is strengthened by the maintenance of historical memory about the conquest of Siberia, the revival of Red Arctic symbolism, and the recent enthusiasm of Russian nationalist movements for the Arctic theme. These movements have seized upon the myth of the Far North... [...]

These meta-narratives advance a supposedly comprehensive and teleological explanation of Russia through a master idea – territorial size and location in space are the drivers of Russia's mission in the world, and of the nature of the Russian state and culture."

There's even a book published in Russia – Artur Indzhiev's "The Battle for the Arctic: Will the North Be Russian?" – that describes the "the onset of a sort of Third World War in which a weakened Russia will have to prove its heroism in order to safeguard its rights in the Arctic against aggressive Western powers." You can already start to see this taking place today, where Russia is furiously attempting to defend its Arctic territorial rights within the framework of the UN.

More powerfully, the Arctic is often presented as a way for Russia to "take revenge on history." It's part of a larger school of thought that all of Russia's threats emanate from the South and Russia must seek refuge in the more spiritual North. This is powerful stuff -- even more powerful than the historical "Slavophile vs. Westernizer" conflict that's usually trotted out by Russian scholars to describe the peculiarities of modern Russian identity.

For Russia, developing an "Arctic Mythology" has important political implications. When you're an embattled regime facing an external threat from abroad – as Russia perceives itself to be now – you need to find ways to unite the population around a great idea or a common enemy. And if you can't find the right combination of "bread and circuses" to distract a nation from troubles at home, sometimes you need a new mythology filled with powerful symbols to make sure everyone's on the same page.

If you buy into the idea that Vladimir Putin is a historian with a deep affinity for Russian philosophers such as Alexander Dugin (a big Arctic fan who believes in the aggressive, nationalist idea of Russian polar bears and Russian penguins), the idea of an Arctic Mythology for Russia makes so much sense. Putin is literally combing through Russian history books, finding narratives (and meta-narratives) that will resonate with the people of Russia.

From this perspective, the various narratives that Russia has trotted out over the past 18 months since the annexation of Crimea can be viewed as attempts at creating (or re-creating) a new Russian mythology. All of these mythologies come with their own built-in historic narratives, and as such, are ready-made to serve specific purposes.

The "Novorossiya Project" was an attempt to reclaim the imperial greatness of Russia in places like Ukraine. The "Eurasian Project" was a clear reference to the historical notion that Russia is a vast Eurasian power, bridging both Europe and Asia. The "pivot to China" was a specific application of this idea, seeking to revive the mythology of the Russian Far East and Russia's traditional vacillation between West and East.

You could go on and on – there's the "BRICS Project" which re-imagines Russia as the head of a new multipolar world. There's the "Greater Europe" project, which mythologizes a gigantic Europe stretching from Vladivostok to Lisbon, by way of Moscow. And there's the "Russian World" project, which seeks to extend the notion of "Russian identity to a global audience.

Within this context, then, the "Arctic Project" is just another attempt to rally the Russian people around a specific notion – that

Russia has always been an Arctic power, and is just now reaffirming its historical role.

The Arctic, in short, is Russia's destiny. All that remains is for this Arctic Mythology to get blended into the Kremlin's current propaganda mix.

Obviously, when you're talking about the Arctic, there are a lot of potential goodies involved – more oil and new trade routes – and this new mythology could galvanize the Russian people the way the concept of the "Wild West" galvanized great American explorers to extend the boundaries of a young nation. If it's just about oil and trade, this mythology makes a lot of sense, and could even serve as a sort of fiscal stimulus for a tottering economy.

However, if the West continues to view Russia's Arctic strategy as just a pretext to extend Russian military might to the High North, gobble up more territory and put a little scare into NATO – all while stirring up a nationalist frenzy at home - then it could end up the way the "Novorossiya Project" turned out – as a true frozen conflict with no winners, only losers.

Beware the Russian boogeyman

Concerns about Russian moves in the Arctic are just the beginning. Russia's military strikes in Syria have unleashed a new bout of scary Russian conspiracy stories in the Western media, just as Russia's annexation of Crimea in 2014 resulted in anxious concerns that Russia was attempting to reclaim the entire former Soviet Union, starting with Ukraine and the Baltic States.

For the Western media, Putin is now the ultimate James Bond villain, concocting a number of evil plots inside the Kremlin to bring down the entire free world. The ability of his super-secret missiles capable of flying 1,000 miles across multiple nations to hit ISIS targets in Syria has people suddenly fearing that Russia is holding back its laser tanks and death rays for Western Europe. At the very least, Russian bombers flying over Syrian airspace are going to cause mid-air collisions with U.S. bombers and launch World War III.

There's a lot that the Russian boogeyman is capable of doing.

The *New York Times*, for example, is now pushing the ultimate cyber war scenario: a plot by Russian submarines to cut the world's undersea Internet cables and lurch the world into digital darkness. It's plausible on a certain level – Russian Internet censorship is a big concern these days, and after seeing Russian President Vladimir Putin dive to the bottom of the sea in a submersible vehicle, it's even possible to imagine that it will be Vladimir Vladimirovich himself doing the actual cutting of the cables.

However, the proof is more circumstantial than real – anything the Russians do these days is suspicious, and submarines lingering near undersea cables makes people nervous. There's even been a panicked report by the U.S. Pentagon that the Russians might actually contemplate a cyber first strike to take out the Internet if there's a war in Europe. Remember, we live in the era of phantom Russian submarines in Sweden and Russian bombers buzzing London, so anything is believable these days.

And, not to be outdone, The Daily Beast has been trumpeting a bizarre alliance between the Kremlin and Taliban in Afghanistan (complete with the image of a AK47-toting Taliban guy in front of St. Basil's). The core of the idea makes sense – Russia wants to crush ISIS and is deathly afraid of radical Islam spreading to its borders in Central Asia. The smart money says that Russia is already covertly funding the Tajiks to deal with ISIS.

But a pact with the Taliban? That would be a pact with the devil, even worse than a pact with Hitler. Anyone remember the Molotov-Ribbentrop Pact from 1939? Remember, it was the Afghan mujahedeen funded by the U.S. to fight the Soviets who eventually became the Taliban. So a partnership with the Taliban would mean that the Russians would be partnering with the very same people who booted them out of Afghanistan during the Cold War? In a world filled with Al-Qaeda, the Taliban and ISIS, it's hard to decide which is the least of the three evils.

If that's not enough to throw a scare into you this Halloween, how about a Russian plot to build military bases in the Arctic in preparation for World War III?

Or maybe you'd prefer a plot by Russia and Iran to divide up the Middle East, including much of Iraq?

Or, even better, a plot by Russia to take over much of the world and form The Third Empire?

Or if Stalinist conspiracies are more your thing, how about a plot by the Kremlin to liquidate the entrepreneurial class, the way Stalin liquidated the kulak class?

And, of course, there's the old standby – Russia partnering with China to crush the West and upend the entire geopolitical order.

If all else fails – trot out the "War Scare of 1983" as proof of the crazy stuff that the paranoid leaders in the Kremlin are capable of doing. During the Cold War, apparently, the Kremlin leadership really and truly believed that the Americans were planning to launch a nuclear first strike against the Soviet Union. That's a pretty chilling notion, especially since the folks in charge of the Kremlin today have extensive roots in the old KGB days of the Soviet Union.

The grain of truth in all these conspiracy plots, of course, is that Russia really, really wants to change the narrative about Ukraine. You could cynically read the entire Russian military intervention in Syria as just a cynical way to shift the topic of conversation. Who can worry about Ukraine, Russia seems to be saying, when there's mayhem breaking out in the Middle East?

The danger, of course, is that people making decisions in the White House and Pentagon start to believe all these conspiracy rumors. You don't need to watch "John Wick" to believe in the Russian boogeyman.

Tili, tili, bom. Close your eyes now. Someone's walking outside the house. And knocks on the door. Tili, tili, bom. The night birds are chirping. He is already inside. To visit those who cannot sleep. He's coming... Closer!

Maybe Russia's Bizarro World is not so bizarre after all

It's hard to deny that modern geopolitics have become Bizarro World ever since Russia intervened in Crimea. Step by step, Vladimir Putin's Russia is creating an alternate universe of new institutions, systems and global partnerships that, in many ways, appears to be the exact opposite of what the West has been offering the world ever since the breakup of the former Soviet Union.

In this Bizarro World, the EU is no longer the only economic option for the fledgling countries of the former Soviet Union — there's now the Eurasian Economic Union (EEU), which is basically a political and economic amalgam of Russia and its two most loyal satellite states — Belarus and Kazakhstan. At least, for now - plans are to recombine other post-Soviet states, like Armenia and Azerbaijan, sometime soon down the road, and that, of course, has people worrying about a reconstitution of the old Soviet Union. (Especially given the recent events in Crimea and eastern Ukraine.) Most likely, though, it's intended as just a way to link Europe and Asia, with Russia as middleman.

Or, take the standard of liberal democracy that the U.S. has been pitching to its allies in Europe, the Middle East and Asia for the almost 25 years since the dissolution of the Soviet Union. Russia is countering with its own brand of political philosophy known as Eurasianism, which relies a lot on the idea that Russia is a unique civilization capable of competing with the West. It suggests that strong moral values matter and that Europe's Atlanticists have somehow lost their footing in the modern world. The growth of

Eurasianism, in short, is the result of turning on the TV and seeing a bearded Austrian transvestite become the new singing sensation of the world.

Russia is also ripping up the playbook when it comes to all the institutions of the modern economic world, like the G8. (Mostly because they've been kicked out of these institutions!) They're working on a separate side deal with other BRICS, working for a way to create a new multipolar world. And they're doing it with a political appeal that makes intuitive sense—that the modern world needs a greater voice for emerging giants like Brazil, India, China and South Africa.

But that's not all.

There's a plan to replace the U.S. dollar with a new reserve currency, thereby breaking up de facto U.S. control of the global financial system. Russia and China recently signed their first agreement on conducting deals with their own national currencies. They're referring to it as the "de-dollarization" of the world.

In fact, in Bizarro World, the modern financial system is going to look very different. There's now a plan afoot to replace the world's most famous ratings agencies—Fitch, S&P and Moody's—with a brand new ratings agency that has both Russian and Chinese backing. Now just trying to downgrade Russian sovereign debt to below investment grade...

The Internet, too, is going to get a brand new look. In some ways, this is a reaction to the whole Snowden Affair. In other ways, it's a response to the growth in unruly dissent made possible by the Web. The Ru-Net ("Russian Internet) has been growing in size in recent years, and now there are plans afoot to get rid of all the big U.S. players and replace them with homegrown favorites. There's a "Russian Google" (Yandex) and a "Russian Facebook" (vKontakte). And there's even a YotaPhone, a "kooky" Russian mobile phone with two screens meant to compete with the iPhone.

And what about GPS for your mobile device or in-vehicle navigation device? Russia has a competing version of GPS called Glonass, as well as a plan to set up Glonass satellite stations across America. That, of course, isn't going to go over so well with American legislators. But then again, Russia is making noise about its unwillingness to support GPS on its own soil as well. So we'll call this one a draw for now.

Speaking of swapping out old Western technologies for new Russian technologies, thought Boeing and Airbus were the only two consortia capable of manufacturing commercial airplanes? Well, China and Russia just signed a deal in Shanghai to create a Bizarro version of Boeing. The plan is to start churning out Ilyushin Dreamliners sometime soon.

And speaking of outer space, Russia is now hinting its support for the international space station program is going to evaporate soon, and that the U.S. could soon be forced to send its astronauts to the space station with a trampoline. Russia, meanwhile, is building a gleaming new space center in the Far East, capable of sending Russian rockets (and cosmonauts) into space without needing to rely on either the U.S. or Europe.

We'll have to see where this brave new adventure to Bizarro World takes us. Russia claims that its alternatives are better suited to the world around us. But are they? Remember the "Seinfeld" episode where Elaine meets new versions of all of her friends in Bizarro World and concludes that she'd rather have the old, lovable characters back, warts and all? That may be the case if the world takes a trip to Russia's Bizarro World and then must make a decision of whether it wants its old Western world back.

Hybrid War

"Never fight against Russians. Your every cunning will be responded by their unpredictable stupidity."

- Otto von Bismarck (1815-1898)

Five ways the Ukraine crisis should remind you of the start of World War I

From the importance of media propaganda in shaping diplomatic thinking to the prevalence of bipolar strategic thinking, the current Ukraine crisis bears an uncanny resemblance to the start of World War I almost exactly a century ago. That's the big takeaway after reading Cambridge historian Christopher Clark's authoritative account of the events that eventually led to the outbreak of World War I, "The Sleepwalkers: How Europe Went to War in 1914."

A close reading of Clark's "The Sleepwalkers" and the events surrounding the start of World War I should be a wake-up call for politicians, analysts and diplomats in both Russia and the West. Indeed, in spring 2015, Graham Allison and Dimitri Simes argued in a cover story for *The National Interest* that Russia and the West are "stumbling to war," much as the Entente and Triple Alliance powers did in 1914. The thought of a military conflict engulfing all of continental Europe was unthinkable at the time, but it quickly became inevitable. We might now also be "sleepwalking" into a conflict with Russia.

Central to Clark's "sleepwalking to war" thesis is something that he refers to as the "Balkan inception scenario," which basically refers to the ability of an isolated political event transpiring in the Balkans having the ability to drag in every major European power as part of a continental conflict. In such a scenario, tensions between Austria-Hungary and one of the Balkan powder keg nations (Serbia, Albania, Montenegro, Bulgaria, Romania) had the potential to drag in Russia, which was bound to France by terms of the Franco-Russian pact. Once France was pulled in, that would pull in Germany, which would then force Great Britain into the fray, as part of an intricate series of diplomatic treaties:

"By the spring of 1914, the Franco-Russian Alliance had constructed a geopolitical trigger along the Austro-Serbian frontier," writes Clark. "They had tied the defense policy of three of the world's greatest powers to the uncertain fortunes of Europe's most violent and unstable region."

So it's no surprise what eventually happened in summer of 1914. The assassination by Serbian nationalists of Franz Ferdinand, Archduke of Austria, on June 28, 1914 forced Austria-Hungary's hand against Serbia. Once Serbia received a de facto ultimatum, it forced Russia to intercede. Then, once Russia mobilized for war, it set into motion matching mobilizations from France and Germany. From there, Europe was at a point of no return. War was inevitable.

Much the same logic applies to today's Europe. But now the current focus of attention is north of the Balkans, to the Baltic States, where Estonia, Latvia and Lithuania actively fear a military invasion from Russia. The Baltic States are especially important because they are bound to NATO by a formal defense guarantee, something that Ukraine lacks. This is the same geopolitical tripwire as the one in 1914. In one scenario that has been much debated, a Russian invasion of a Russian-speaking enclave in Estonia or Latvia might trigger the military involvement of NATO. From there, it would be a point of no return.

Another point that Clark makes early in his monumental historical work (Chapter 3, "The Polarization of Europe: 1887–1907") is that the fundamental problem facing Europe in 1914 was the onset of two formal blocs facing off against each other. On one side, you had Russia, France and Great Britain. On the other side, you had Austria-Hungary, Germany and (to a certain extent) Italy. This marked a fundamental change from the earlier 1880s period, when a multipolar arrangement dominated. In 1887, for example, Russia was tied to Germany by means of the Reinsurance Treaty, but had not yet developed the Franco-Russian Alliance or the Anglo-Russian convention.

With a multi-polar arrangement, there is much greater ability to defuse a crisis. One act against another state does not immediately compel allies to rush to their defense.

"The polarization of Europe's geopolitical system was a crucial precondition for the war that broke out in 1914. It is almost impossible to see how a crisis in Austro-Serbian relations, however grave, could have dragged the Europe of 1887 into a continental war," according to Clark. "The bifurcation into two alliance blocs did not cause the war; indeed it did as much to mute as to escalate conflict in the pre-war years. Yet without the two blocs, the war could not have broken out in the way that it did. The bipolar system structured the environment in which the crucial decisions were made."

That's what makes today's security arrangement in Europe so threatening. You have two rival blocs — Russia vs. NATO (and, for that matter, the EU vs. the EEU). The only way to change the bipolar system in Europe is either to bring in peripheral powers such as Turkey to widen the European project or to erode the EU completely by splintering off European nations (Hungary, Greece,

Italy) that might be amenable to a Russian rapprochement. To solve today's Ukraine crisis, multipolar thinking has to replace dangerous bipolar thinking.

Another theme that Clark elaborates on at length (and especially in Chapter 12, "Last Days") is something that might be best referred to as the tension between "imperialist" and "continentalist" perspectives. On one hand, European powers had to worry about their strategic position within continental Europe. On the other hand, they had to worry about their imperial possessions abroad.

As a result, actions taken in places such as Persia, Mongolia, Turkey or Morocco had the potential to reverberate throughout Europe. Germany, lacking a significant imperial presence abroad (at least, compared to France, Great Britain and Russia), greatly feared that it was being boxed in and restrained in its future economic ambitions.

In the same way today, there are echoes of the fundamental tensions between imperialist and continentalist viewpoints in how we talk about the Ukraine crisis. Russian cooperation in resolving the Ukraine crisis, for example, is often tied to cooperation on global issues, such as Syria, Iran or ISIS.

Just as Europe in 1914 could not discuss Serbia without discussing the impact of the Balkans on their imperial ambitions, today's European powers cannot discuss Ukraine without discussing the impact of Donetsk and Luhansk on their strategic goals in the Middle East and Asia.

Clark also highlights the power of media narratives to limit diplomatic alternatives. We often think of today's "information war" between Russia and the West as being somehow unique, a first in world history. Yet, jump back 100 years ago, and the same type of information war was being waged across Europe. Close links between diplomatic staff and the media made it possible to insert narratives into newspapers that could activate entire populations, either for or against war. Clark even uses the word "propaganda" (so fashionable today) to describe some of the media efforts being used across Europe (not just Russia).

And, writes Clark in Chapter 6 ("Last Chances: Détente and Danger, 1912–1914"), these media narratives often came back to limit the policy options of politicians and diplomats, who realized too late how hard it was to buck public opinion and take a position that would be unfavorable to the broader population. To take but just one example, consider how the power of media narratives shaped the way Germany and Russia viewed each other in the period leading up to World War I. The following passage is from Clark:

"[The Liman von Sanders affair] showed, firstly, how belligerent the thinking of some of the Russian policy-makers had become. [Russian Foreign Minister Sergey] Sazonov in particular had moved from the vacillations of his early period in office towards a firmer and more Germanophobic stance—he had begun to construct a narrative of German-Russian relations that left no room for an understanding with Berlin: Russia had always been the docile, peace-loving neighbor and Germany the duplicitous predator, bullying and humiliating the Russians at every opportunity. Now the time had come to stand firm! The power of such narratives to shrink policy horizons should not be underestimated."

Sound familiar? This sounds almost exactly like the same narrative that Russia is constructing now about Germany, just substitute "Lavrov" for "Sazonov" and "the MH17 Affair" for "The Liman von Sanders affair" and there's almost a complete match.

Finally, Clark highlights the complete failure of predicting diplomatic outcomes based on the actions or thoughts of a single person. It's fashionable in 2015 to talk about the diplomatic strategies of nations as if they are the work of a single person or a limited group of insiders. We talk about "Putin's Russia" or "Putin's regime," as if Russian President Vladimir Putin had full ability and knowledge to control every act of Russia abroad. We portray the Ukraine standoff as a personal confrontation between Obama and Putin, or between Merkel and Putin.

Nothing could be further from the truth. What makes Clark's research on World War I so staggering is how he goes deep into the historical archives—examining telegrams, diaries and official correspondence—to see what national sovereigns and foreign ministers were doing on the eve of World War I.

What he found is shocking—most sovereigns had little or no idea of what was really happening, and foreign ministers routinely attempted to dominate national cabinets and exclude top officials from any discussion of war or military strategy—or to even notify them of the existence of treaties and alliances.

Even within political parties, the amount of infighting was incomprehensible—you get the impression from reading Clark that politicians in every country were actively sabotaging each other's efforts and, only in the end, realized how tragically everything would turn out.

That's why it's such a mistake to view Russia solely through the Putin prism. It may yet turn out that Vladimir Putin was the most sober-minded individual within Russia advocating for a steadier hand in Ukraine, as opposed to the views of Russia's super-hawks. As a result, turning the Ukraine crisis into the justification for regime change in Russia might end up being one of the worst things ever.

Thomas Graham of Kissinger Associates, in an op-ed for the *Financial Times*, recently wrote that, "Europe's problem is with Russia, not with Putin." Predicting outcomes based on a single person or a single personality may work in the short-term, but never in the long-term.

In short, the crisis in Ukraine has reached a dangerous new phase. So many of the warning signals of today echo those of a bygone era, when the perfidious work of Serbian nationalists set off one of the worst tragedies in the history of Western civilization. Those acts of 100 years ago have implications for today: Those who do not remember the past are condemned to repeat it.

Ukraine, the first postmodern war

Imagine a war without beginning or end, a perpetual flow of low-intensity information and economic warfare, rapidly-shifting coalitions within and between nations, and a perpetual fog of war that obfuscates not just the aims of those fighting, but even those doing the fighting.

That is the situation now in Ukraine. The events surrounding the Ukraine crisis might echo those of a bygone era – World War I – but the ebb and flow of events is distinctly postmodern.

It would be too simplistic to call this a war of Russia vs. the West, or even a war of Moscow vs. Kiev. This is not a hot war and it is not a cold war. It is not a clash of one civilization against another civilization. It is, as British political philosopher Thomas Hobbes once suggested, a war of all against all.

And in this first postmodern war, truth is relative, not absolute. It can be glimpsed, but it cannot be apprehended.

At a time of unmatched technological innovation, it is almost inconceivable that NATO – the mightiest military alliance in the history of the world – is relying on second-hand satellite images from a private company in Colorado for proof of a Russian "invasion." Digital ephemera – YouTube videos, Facebook status updates and Instagram selfies of Russian soldiers - are now worth more than all the intelligence-gathering capabilities of the world's most vaunted defense ministries and intelligence agencies.

The concept of Ukraine as the world's postmodern war can actually be traced back to a short work of fiction – "Without the

Sky" - that appeared in Russia in March 2014 around the time that Russia took back Crimea. The author was Vladislav Surkov (using the pseudonym Natan Dubovitsky) – the same Vladislav Surkov who is a long-time ideological adviser to Vladimir Putin. Surkov ended up on the Western sanctions list and, in defiance, described himself as a fan of both Tupac Shakur and Jackson Pollock -- but not of America.

To understand Surkov's postmodernist story in its full brilliance, one needs to read it in the original Russian, although descriptions of the themes from the story have appeared in both *Foreign Policy* and *The Economist*. As Surkov explains, this new form of postmodernist warfare will be "a non-linear war" – a type of warfare that is now typically described as "hybrid warfare."

And that helps to explain why the West has had such a difficult time making sense of Russia's actions in Ukraine.

One of the more surreal aspects of the current crisis in Ukraine is how quickly so-called Russia experts embraced the old Cold War narrative of West vs. East and Europe vs. Russia. Back came all the old, tired Cold War tropes. Ukraine as a Cold War redux? Nothing could be further from the truth – the West is fractured between Europe and the U.S., Europe is fractured between those who need Russian gas and those who do not, and Ukraine is fractured between West and East. In a globalized, hyper-connected world, Cold Wars as we used to know them are no longer possible.

As a result, Surkov calls this a "non-linear" war, comprised of coalitions with different interests. It is no longer one side against one side, or two-against-two, or even three-against-one. It is all-against-all:

"Это была первая нелинейная война. В примитивных войнах девятнадцатого, двадцатого и других средних веков дрались обычно две стороны. Две нации или два временных союза. Теперь столкнулись четыре коалиции. И не то, что двое на двое. Или трое против одного. Нет. Все против всех."

And, to top it off, these coalitions - even coalitions within nations - are constantly shifting and changing sides:

"И что это были за коалиции! Не такие, как раньше. Редкие государства входили в них целиком. Случалось, несколько провинций выступали на одной стороне, несколько на другой, а какой-нибудь город или поколение, или пол, или профессиональное сообщество того же государства - на третьей. Потом они могли переменить положение. Перейти в какой угодно лагерь. Иногда прямо в бою."

Consider that, within Ukraine, it is almost impossible to tell the origin of those doing the fighting. Little green men? Separatists? Terrorists? Rebels? Mercenaries from Chechnya? Russian regulars on vacation? And what about all the small-time Ukrainian oligarchs who stand to carve out their own feudal kingdoms in return for helping Kiev?

This is a war where the ultimate goal is not "victory" but, rather, the "process of war." War historically has meant the achievement of some goal – the pursuit of territory or treasure. No longer:

"Простодушные полководцы прошлого стремились к победе. Теперь поступали не так глупо. То есть, некоторые, конечно, держались старых обычаев. И пытались вытащить из архивов туманные заклинания. Типа победа будет за нами. Местами срабатывало. Но в основном понимали войну как процесс. Точнее, часть процесса, острую его фазу. Не самую, может быть, важную."

As some have recently suggested, Ukraine is turning into a war where the goal is not so much "victory" as to create a "frozen conflict" that can be defrosted, re-heated and warmed up as needed to achieve political goals. Maybe it means keeping Ukraine from joining NATO, maybe it means weakening the authorities in Kiev or bringing about regime change in Moscow, or maybe it means delivering on domestic promises at home.

Finally, this is a war that takes place silently overhead, while raining down destruction on those below. Surkov describes this as a world where "absolutely silent machines" go to war against each other, high up in the sky:

"Мы помним, как с четырех сторон на наше небо слетелись четыре великие армады. Это не были ревущие, свистящие и воющие летательные аппараты старого образца, какие мы привыкли видеть в видеохронике. Впервые применялась новейшая, абсолютно бесшумная техника. С какими-то невиданными системами полного звукопоглощения. Сотнитысяч самолетов, вертолетов, ракет уничтожали друг друга весь день. В гробовой тишине. Даже падая, они молчали."

You can take this as an allegory for the economic and information war that is taking place silently in the digital ether. This may be the first war in history where the combined scope of "information war" and "economic war" exceeds the level of military escalation. Armies line up and then abandon positions before fighting. Mercenaries fade into the landscape. Meanwhile, Western diplomats continue to dream up economic sanctions that magically target only a limited number of individuals, organizations or sectors.

As with any postmodernist work, a postmodern war comes with widely divergent narratives and interpretations. And any vestige of postmodernism is rejected by those clinging to modernism. What some claim is a 19th century style of warfare may actually turn out to be a 21st century style of warfare. We just don't recognize it as such yet.

We used to call these widely divergent narratives and interpretations "propaganda" – now we call them "branding" or "PR" or (most stylishly) "optics." For every CNN in New York, there is a Channel One in Moscow. For every RT (formerly known as Russia Today), there is a Ukraine Today.

As a result, media in the West and in Russia show vastly different images. The U.S. shows images of masked, heavily armed separatists wielding missile launchers. Russia shows scenes of total destruction in cities like Luhansk and Donetsk, refugees streaming across the border, and scenes of nationalist groups marauding through Ukrainian cities. Both play, on an endless loop, nearly 24/7, on our computer screens and TV monitors.

It is impossible not to have an emotional response. In the West, of course, one is reminded of Orwell's "1984" and the Ministry of Truth, which, it turns out, is really a Ministry of Propaganda. There are surely other stories where the truth is just as malleable. The West has Orwell's "1984," Russia has Zamyatin's dystopian "We."

In this war, every side seems to have a Ministry of Truth. As a result, truth is no longer an absolute, especially in the era of the Internet. Warfare is now photoshopped and carefully edited to go viral. Nothing can be ascertained for certain, so everything can be denied. Ordinary citizens do as they are told as governments prepare to battle over concepts they do not truly understand.

All of the conditions described by Surkov in "Without the Sky" have fallen into place. There are four coalitions – the West, Ukraine, the separatists and Russia. There is a constant flow of low-intensity informational and economic warfare taking place in the digital ether around us and above us. And there is no chance to achieve ultimate "victory" – only the chance for an endless "frozen conflict" in which innocents pay the final price. It is truly a postmodern war.

While some claim that the Vietnam War was the first "postmodern" war, it is only in Ukraine that the world has seen what real postmodern war looks like in the Internet era. Attempting to understand what is really going on in Ukraine is similar to the feeling that one gets when attempting to understand a great work of art that has arrived before its time. There is a struggle to recognize the old in the new before realizing that the old no longer exists.

Just remember the world's reaction to Picasso's postmodernist "Guernica" nearly 75 years ago, which depicted the brutal shelling of a 1930s Spanish village by the Nazis and Italian fascists in jagged cubist and abstract forms.

It was a statement about the brutality and randomness of war like we had never seen before and is generally considered to be one of the greatest anti-war statements ever. Will we need an Internet Picasso constructing a new digital "Guernica" from pixilated scenes in Kiev or Donetsk or Luhansk to convince us once again of the horrors of war?

MH17, the Guernica of the Ukraine crisis

In many ways, the shoot down of Flight MH17 over Ukraine in July 2014 was the ultimate postmodernist act in the ultimate postmodernist war. The MH17 tragedy quickly became a new "Guernica" to remind us of the horrors of hybrid war. Only, in this case, the artist's canvas was the pixilated computer screen, where reality and unreality are combining in strange ways to determine the future narrative of the Ukraine crisis.

Consider that there are at least eight different storylines about the Malaysian plane crash perpetuated by the Western media that are either unproven – or, at worst, downright untrue. All of them have helped to change the narrative of events in Ukraine and alter the way the world views Russia.

If you're like most Americans, you probably spent the better part of a week in July 2014 following the gripping saga of the MH17 plane crash either via TV or social media. Maybe you skipped past mainstream news channels like CNN and MSNBC and tuned in to Al-Jazeera. Maybe you tried to find out first-hand what the Russian media was actually saying about all this.

But let's face it – even more than one year later, nobody has any conclusive proof of what actually happened. The Americans still blame the Russians, the Ukrainians still blame the separatists, and the Russians still blame the Ukrainians.

Even after the Dutch Safety Board released its findings on the tragedy in October 2015, the results were not conclusive. During the same week, the Russians released their own version of the Dutch report, and as might be expected, these results seemed to exonerate the separatists and place the blame on the Ukrainian military.

It's a mess – and given the need for American cable TV and social media to provide a running commentary on any disaster 24/7 – there's bound to be a lot speculation and rootless commentary mixed in with fact, and that's how a lot of controversial storylines about MH17 emerged.

The problem, quite simply, is that the fog of war that characterized the first phase of the Ukraine crisis transformed ominously into the impenetrable smoke of a downed commercial airliner and the flaming wreckage of a Boeing 777 that claimed nearly 300 innocent lives.

The major thesis of the Western media narrative is that the pro-Russian separatists have something to hide and are making it impossible for crash investigators to get to the scene. This was the running storyline in the media most days – various talking heads implying that investigators indiscriminately imposed a series of random checkpoints across Eastern Ukraine and seriously impeded the ability of any international observers to get to the scene.

President Obama, in his remarks to the nation, also implied this. Yet is this actually the case? Russian Foreign Minister Sergey Lavrov has pointed out again and again that international observers were on the scene, and that all attempts were made to make this a traditional air crash investigation, in accordance with all international norms.

The Western media also suggested that the black box and the BUK missile launcher were found by the separatists and immediately shipped to Moscow. Again, this is a fact rejected by the Russian Foreign Ministry. Sergey Lavrov pointedly noted that Moscow does not want, and is not in possession of, the black box from MH17.

To discredit the Russian side, the Western media repeatedly emphasized that Russian media is completely under the control of the Kremlin and is now busy cranking out its own version of the events.

One version of the events, mentioned more than once on CNN, is that Russian media created a storyline in which the missile was actually fired by the Ukrainian army and was an attempt to take out the plane of President Vladimir Putin on his flight back to Russia. The bizarreness of this story, of course, is used to show that all Russian media is essentially "propaganda," and hence, untrustworthy. (But any more bizarre than the thesis, given airtime in the West, including by CNN, that the MH17 tragedy was part of a Russian plot engineered by Vladimir Putin to bring the airplane to a commodore in Kazakhstan?)

There have even been attempts to link MH17 with earlier events from the era of the Soviet Union, the so-called "Evil Empire." Western media immediately said that we could expect the same behavior from Russia now as when the Soviet Union covered up the Korean Air Lines (KAL) downed airliner story in 1983. The problem, quite simply, is that we didn't hear or see any Russian sources on TV, so we assumed that the Russians were hiding behind the facts, trying to find a way to make this story go away.

And it doesn't help that a Cold Warrior like John McCain received a lot of airtime, sharing his Cold War mentality with the media. He, surely, still believes that the Soviet Union and Pravda are alive and well.

Western media has also insinuated that Russian President Vladimir Putin is somehow personally behind the missile attack – and can also somehow personally end the violence in Eastern Ukraine. Sadly, this is the storyline that emerges just about any time there's a story about Russia's involvement in Ukraine.

Yet, as some analysts have pointed out, the efforts at "plausible deniability" (in which Russia aids covertly, but not overtly, the separatists) have led to a difficult situation for Russia, in which some elements may have gone "rogue."

The Kremlin may have lost its grip on exactly what is happening in Eastern Ukraine. So when the White House warns that "Putin better bring an end to the violence, or else!" – they better be sure that he really can bring an end to the violence.

To establish the broader media narrative, amateur YouTube videos, audio recordings posted online, theories from "unnamed" sources and deleted tweets are allowable evidence against the Russians. In the information vacuum that occurred in the 24 to 48 hours after the tragedy, people hunted for any proof – no matter how outlandish - for who (and what) caused the airliner crash.

They posted YouTube videos from Eastern Ukraine, discovered purported calls made between evil separatists at the moment they realize the airliner wasn't a Ukrainian transport plane, and pointed to deleted tweets from Igor Strelkov and other separatists, who appear to brag of bringing down Ukrainian planes.

"Unnamed officials" – no doubt, the same unnamed officials who had no idea that Russia was planning on getting involved in Crimea – suddenly are sure beyond a shadow of a doubt that a Russian missile brought down the plane. Yet, keep in mind, even CNN has added a caveat to most everything it shows about MH17, a version of "We have no way of verifying this information."

So why is the Western media narrative about MH17 so much more effective than the Russian media narrative about MH17? That's an easy question to answer - people speaking in English to reporters on cable news TV are more reliable than people who don't. This is one of those white elephants in the middle of the room that people don't want to talk about.

Consider for a moment the following: the "good guys" in Kiev dress in suits and speak English, while the "bad guys" in Donetsk have their phone conversations subtitled in English and are usually seen in file photos wearing army fatigues or dressed in masks.

To the casual observer, the subtext is clear: people who act like the West, dress like the West and speak like the West must be friendly to the West. And vice versa. (This should remind you a lot of the Russian-Georgian war of 2008, when the Georgians used this approach to win over Western media, and then Western policymakers).

To establish that modern Russia is a new Evil Empire, it's important to establish that the attack on the airliner was entirely unprovoked. Again, patently untrue, when you consider the attacks that the Ukrainian army have been carrying out in Eastern Ukraine as a renewal of the campaign against the separatists.

Bombing campaigns against villages convinced the separatists that they needed to get their hands on more advanced military equipment, not the other way around. For weeks before MH17, the Russians were trying to show Western observers the damage and destruction caused by the attacks by Ukrainian government forces.

As a result of this Western media narrative, this plane crash is going to remain a global PR nightmare for Russia. At the very least, people in the West (especially the Dutch and the Aussies) aren't going to have any willingness to trust Russia on anything for a long time.

Already, the same cable TV guests who were once calling the pro-Russian forces in Ukraine "separatists" are now calling them "militants." Soon, they will be doing what the Ukrainians are doing, and that's calling them "bastards" and "terrorists."

Russia needed to get somebody on TV and social media talking about this – and not just the venerable Stephen F. Cohen, who's already been on Al-Jazeera - or the Ukrainians are going to own the narrative about the event, just like the Georgians did back in 2008. Remember, this was an information war before it became a shooting war. Now it threatens to become a disinformation war.

From the masked girls of Pussy Riot to the masked men of Ukraine

As Vladislav Surkov suggests in his fictional work "Without the Sky," the lines dividing different coalitions in any postmodern war are blurry at best. That extends to coalitions within states as well as coalitions between states. Within Russia, for example, the lines between "democrat," "nationalist," "separatist," and "patriot" are rarely clear for Russia's post-perestroika generation.

Even Russian opposition figures are often just members of the so-called "systemic opposition" – the opposition that is allowed by the Kremlin to give the appearance of a Western democracy in action. Within Russia, the appearance of any new opposition party is widely suspected of just being part of a Kremlin operation, created to siphon votes away from real opposition figures.

Anyone in the U.S. attempting to understand the political consciousness of the modern Russia—and that includes officials in the U.S. State Department and members of Congress in Washington—would do well to pick up Zakhar Prilepin's mega-cult novel "Sankya."

The novel, which has been hugely popular in Russia ever since it was published in 2006, is finally available in English translation and comes with a slim foreword that was written by popular Russian opposition leader Alexei Navalny during his highly-controversial bid to become Moscow mayor in 2013.

Two epic scenes serve to bookend this testosterone-filled, vodka-soaked novel. In the first chapter, young Russian protesters chanting anti-government slogans run wild in the center of Moscow, turning over foreign cars and smashing windows. In the final chapter, the same protesters have joined up with a disillusioned, head-butting OMON dropout to loot a military ammunition dump, strap on full-body armor, and seize government buildings before they're forced to stand down in the face of overwhelming firepower from the Russian authorities. These two scenes can be thought of as a fictionalized Bolotnaya and Donetsk, two touchstone events in the transformation of the opposition movement from a purely Russian phenomenon into a post-Soviet phenomenon.

In between, we meet some of the faces of the Russian protest movement, here called The Founders. (This is a group that has significantly more in common with the National Bolshevik and Right Sector movements than with the young generation of Muscovites who rallied to Bolotnaya, but more of that later.)

There's Sasha ("Sankya") Tishin, the titular hero of the book, who appears to be desperately looking for some purpose in a life that is nasty, brutish and short. He keeps telling his mother that he's OK, even when the Russian FSB is busting down doors of Moscow apartments, trying to find him. There's Yana, a beautiful young female leader of the movement who sounds like a dead-ringer for Nadya Tolokonnikova of Pussy Riot. She delights in political hooliganism and committing nonsensical acts against the Russian authorities, all while exclaiming, "This was a political action!"

There's also Kostenko—the revered leader of the Founders who seems to be the personification of Eduard Limonov of the National Bolsheviks. And then there are a whole host of supporting characters—Matvey, Nega, Posik, Rogov, and Verochka—who do their share to supply the opposition movement with guns, vodka and ideas for a never-ending supply of stunts to aggravate the Russian security forces. In the book, often they become mini-celebrities as their faces flash momentarily on independent Russian TV stations broadcasting their acts of defiance against the Russian state.

The Russian-language version of "Sankya" has been downloaded almost 300,000 times since it was published. It has won literary prizes and has even been turned into an award-winning theatrical play called "Thugs." A back cover blurb for the book references Tolstoy, but a more fitting comparison would be Gorky—this is not a book to be consumed in a university classroom, it's a book to be read in the streets while contemplating revolution.

At its core, "Sankya" can be seen as the most vivid explanation of how we went from Pussy Riot to Bolotnaya, and then from Maidan to Donetsk in a span of just a few years. In other words, how Russian society went from Pussy Riot to the masked men of Eastern Ukraine.

And, not surprising, given the celebrity status of Prilepin in Russia these days and the types of events depicted within the book (in one, Yana throws an egg at the Russian president, thus triggering the full-on wrath of the authorities and the unexplained death of two of the top Founders), the book has also attracted the attention of Vladimir Putin and one of his former top advisors, Vladislav Surkov. Dmitry Medvedev, when asked to name one contemporary Russian writer who's a must-read, mentioned Zakhar Prilepin.

And that's where things get interesting, since the book—more than any other that currently exists in print in the English language—portrays the fundamental tension that exists within post-Soviet society today. Even if it was written in 2006 for a specifically Russian milieu, it feels as topical today, given the recent events in Ukraine and Moldova.

Navalny nails it in the foreword, when he writes:

"Prilepin has not merely turned inside out the consciousness of the entire post-Perestroika generation of politicized young Russians and laid it bare, but also, in large part, predicted the patterns of development of radical political groups and the government's strategy in combating them."

For this new post-Perestroika generation, the faces of Western-style capitalism are the old Soviet bosses who rigged the system and now have cash, cars and the ear of the president. Meanwhile, they're left to scrape by, unable to afford more than a few shots of cheap vodka and pickled cucumbers while their grandparents rot away at the dacha.

In other words, we're going to continue to see these types of radical opposition movements in Russia, no matter how hard the government cracks down on them, as long as the economics don't improve. What's driving these opposition leaders is not an ideology, per se, but a lack of ideology. Their actions are raw and visceral and filled with a combination of despair and hate, like when they fight a group of ethnic Chechens in a Moscow market, or when they conduct a high-intensity terrorist attack on a McDonald's that leaves charred wreckage behind.

Throughout the novel, characters—like the Afghan war vet missing an arm or the polished liberal opposition figure Bezletov—come and go, challenging these members of the opposition movement to define what they stand for. They stand for nothing other than revolution. They cannot articulate a new future for Russia, and they have no new ideas. They are disillusioned and simply want to strike back at the "vile" and "vulgar" Russian authorities. They are not scared of death.

What's compelling in all this, of course, is how we go from Pussy Riot and Bolotnaya to Maidan and Donetsk within the arc of a single novel. In between, there's a brief interlude in Riga, in which the Founders cause havoc as retribution against the Latvian government. They later hire Sasha to assassinate a judge who's sentenced a few of the founders to 15 years in prison.

This Riga sub-plot, if you will, is the start of how we go from the protest movements as a uniquely Russian phenomenon to a post-Soviet phenomenon. The scope of action intensifies, from throwing eggs and rocks, to Molotov cocktails and Kalashnikovs. It ends with a struggle to the death, the siege of a Russian government building, and plans to extend the fighting to 30 provincial cities.

What to make of all this? More likely, that the composition of the Russian "protest movement" or the "pro-Russian separatist movement" is much more complex and nuanced than we would like to admit. "Patriotism" can be an excuse to cling to power—or an excuse for violent revolution. There's a lost generation in the post-Soviet space, looking for purpose and meaning. Stunts like Maidan and Donetsk—filled with TV cameras willing to glorify their actions—are becoming their new outlet for approval, now that they are cut off from a bright economic future.

That should be disconcerting for anyone who things that the masked men in Ukraine are ever going to just disappear and go away. "Sankya" is literally the soundtrack of the modern Russia, and as Navalny says in the foreword, the "real raw nerve of modern Russian life."

What separatists in Europe can teach us about separatists in Ukraine

The masked separatists of eastern Ukraine may actually have more in common with the separatists of Europe – in places such as Scotland and Catalonia – than the Western media would like to admit.

As new separatist movements appear in Europe – especially Scotland, which just barely missed voting for independence in September 2014, and Catalonia, which voted for independence in September 2015 - that could have interesting implications for the way we think about the separatists in Ukraine and the complex historical relationship between Russia and Ukraine.

The following description, written six months after the annexation of Crimea and just days before the Scots went to the polls to vote for independence from the UK, could have applied equally well to both Scotland and eastern Ukraine:

"Europe could have a new state by the end of the year. Separatists in one corner of Europe appear to be gaining the upper hand in their bid for independence as they tap into complex feelings and emotions that have formed over centuries. If this separatist movement spirals out of control, some fear it could roil the oil markets and raise concerns about nuclear weapons getting into the wrong hands. And that could have enormous implications for NATO, the EU and the way we think about the right to national self-determination across Europe."

The notion of Scotland declaring its independence from the United Kingdom – a surreal dream only a few years ago – suddenly became a very real possibility. According to the latest polls released before the September 2014 vote, 51 percent of Scots (including Sir Sean Connery) favored separation from the United Kingdom. This remarkable turn of events in Scotland – a surge of public support for independence that caught the U.S. napping – could help us understand the crisis in Ukraine in three important ways.

First and most importantly, the situation in Scotland could help us understand why Russia feels the loss of its empire so acutely and why Russia values Ukraine so much. Replace "Scotland" with "Ukraine" and "Great Britain" with "Russia" in any op-ed about the Scottish independence vote and you have a surprisingly spot-on description of what people in Russia feel about Ukraine.

It's easy to see why many Brits weren't so pleased about Scotland's potential rejection of the United Kingdom. Adam Taylor of *The Washington Post* detailed all the ways that losing Scotland could turn out to be exceptionally painful for the Brits – in the same way that losing Ukraine would be exceptionally painful for Russians.

For one, you'd have to change the term "Great Britain" to something like "Little Britain." That hurts. Then, you'd have to create a new flag. In doing so, you'd have to rethink what it means to be British in areas ranging from sports to culture to politics. And you'd have to worry that other constituents of the United Kingdom – like tiny NATO-friendly Wales – might also launch independence movements of their own.

Secondly, the separatist situation in places like Scotland and Catalonia could help Russia watchers to understand that there's a huge difference between calling people "separatists" and "terrorists." Would anybody call people voting for Scottish independence "terrorists"? What happened after the Kiev Maidan was a spiral of violence that's only possible when inherent needs for national self-determination are not being met. All of a sudden a word like "separatists" mutated into "rebels" and "terrorists" in Kiev's proclamations, but no one did the same for Scotland's "rebels."

This is not to suggest that the same chain of events could have happened in Scotland if a vote for independence was somehow subverted – only that something supposedly simple – like Ukraine voting for an Association Agreement with the EU – carries very weighty consequences. In the Scottish example, some people have already speculated that British Prime Minister David Cameron could have been forced out of office if the Scots voted for independence. Who could have seen that coming?

By voting for independence from the United Kingdom, Scotland's separatists are not rejecting capitalism and they are not rejecting London – they just feel that they can do a better job of governing their own affairs. It's all about national identity and cultural pride and regional autonomy.

The same factors – to a much greater and more volatile degree, of course – are at work in Crimea and eastern Ukraine. Yet, we focus on the "little green men" and conspiracy plots hatched in Moscow instead of the hundreds of thousands of displaced Ukrainians who are voting with their feet and moving to Russia.

Finally, Scotland's separatists can help us understand the way forward in Ukraine if the Minsk-2 ceasefire holds. What would a "federalism" solution actually look like – and would it be sustainable? There's a lot for Scotland to work out if it actually does declare independence, everything from how government institutions will work to practical everyday matters like what a Scottish national currency would look like.

And, as Vox pointed out in its Scotland explainer, "Those are just the technical questions – the new government would also need to develop a tax structure, fund its social-welfare platform, and make decisions about immigration and a host of other policy questions."

If all had worked out as the separatists planned, Scotland could have provided a Western-approved template for Ukraine. It could have helped to determine the immediate consequences of granting greater autonomy to regions such as Donetsk and Luhansk. It could provide guidance for bigger, more macro issues – everything from whether or not Ukraine would join NATO and what the border between Russia and Ukraine would look like.

Would it ever be possible to have joint Ukrainian and Russian citizenship? Would Ukraine become monocultural or bicultural?

All of this is really just a thought experiment – like talking about Washington's debt problems in the same terms as if the U.S. were a bankrupt banana republic.

The backers of the Scottish separatist movement claimed that it was a once-in-a-generation vote, and that if the vote fails – they will abandon it once and forever. The ads for the "Yes" and "No" campaigns for independence show prosperous families and housewives, not masked separatists or tent encampments. In short, there is no risk of armed conflict. There is no concern about

London playing a sinister role in Glasgow to squelch independence.

But this thought experiment is nonetheless interesting for showing us what we're not thinking about when we think about Ukraine. We've been so conditioned to thinking about Ukraine through a Cold War filter that we're using the same heuristics as 25 years ago to understand what's going on now in Ukraine.

We see only two rival blocs – NATO vs. Russia – engaged in a winner-take-all confrontation; the reappearance of a new Iron Curtain between Russia and the West; a return of realpolitik in geopolitics; and a clash of civilizations between Russia and Europe.

We instinctively see any vote for independence in Ukraine as a vote between two very different systems (capitalism vs. communism, democracy vs. authoritarianism).

Maybe, just maybe, the Scottish separatist vote or the Catalonian separatist vote will change our views and force us to abandon the old Cold War thinking.

Just as the U.S. was caught napping on Scotland, it was caught napping on Ukraine. From here on out, the new thinking about the parameters of Euro-Atlantic security will have to take into account emerging separatist movements – not just within the former Soviet Union but also within the former United Kingdom and the former EU.

The Syrian hybrid war is Ukraine, part 2

In many ways, the current information war in Syria should remind you of the information war in Ukraine. There are the same sightings of "little green men" (many of them "volunteers"), the same charges that Russia is using state propaganda to provide a massive smokescreen for its role in the campaign, and the same concerns that Russia is waging a very different type of hybrid war in Syria.

However, there's another aspect of this information war that can't be ignored – and that's the blatant amount of disinformation from both sides that's been mixed in with all the information. In short, Syria is not so much an "information war" as a "disinformation war."

And, just as the Russians and the Americans traded accusations over what's happening in Ukraine, the same situation is now taking place in Syria. It's almost an exact replay. It seems that there's nothing the two sides can agree on. Syria is Ukraine, Part 2.

On one hand, you've got the Russian side churning out its version of the events. And on the other hand, you've got the U.S. side churning out its version of events.

What's particularly noteworthy, says Radio Free Europe/Radio Liberty, is how the Kremlin is controlling the media narrative in Syria: "With slickly produced videos, quick-cut drone footage of air strikes, animated graphics, on-the-ground photos, and rapid-response Twitter and Facebook updates, the Kremlin has taken a page from Washington's operations manual, embracing information warfare for the 21st-century media environment."

It's not just the Russian Ministry of Defense, however, that's involved in this information war. The Russian Ministry of Foreign Affairs, via its lovely spokeswoman, Maria Zakharova, has also remained on the offensive, taking exception with the U.S. interpretation of events in Syria -- the claim that Russian warplanes are bombing civilians, the claim that Russian army regulars are involved in ground operations, the claim that Russian warplanes are purposely violating Turkish airspace, and the claim that Russian cruise missiles fired over Iran are killing Iranian cows.

And that was just in the first week of bombing.

Every time the U.S. accuses the Russians of bombing "the moderate opposition," Russia accuses the U.S. of funding moderate opposition groups who have become ISIS terrorists. Russia says it's hitting back against ISIS, the U.S. says Russia is hitting back against the anti-Assad opposition. The Western media even says Russia might be dropping bombs on Chechens as some sort of retribution for the first two Chechen Wars. Russia says its missiles are hitting their targets every time, the U.S. says the missiles aren't hitting their targets.

There's also the matter of where all the Russian munitions are coming from and going to. Just as nobody saw the massive buildup along the Ukraine border before the annexation of Crimea, nobody's seen the massive buildup of the "Syrian Express" – all the planes and boats bringing Russian military supplies to Syria. The best theory to date is that the Russians completed some type of misdirection play in the Caucasus, sending shipments via Iranian and even Iraqi airspace.

Finally, consider the matter of the massive refugee influx into Europe. The U.S. views this refugee crisis as the fault of the abusive, authoritarian regime of Assad in Syria, while Russia views it as the fault of America's destabilizing role in the Middle East.

So how is it possible that the Russians and the Americans can have precisely the opposition spin on events?

You could blame the fog of war. It's not quite clear who's bombing who, and why. It's even harder to tell when cruise missiles are flying 1,000 miles through three different countries (which might explain the Iranian cows).

You could also blame the confusing nature of the Middle East. The UAE Russian Embassy recently tweeted out a cartoon showing about ten different groups of scary looking Syrian rebels, and a tagline along the lines of: "Just who are the moderate opposition?"

But there's a third, more compelling explanation – Russia and the U.S. have two different views of the world. The West is still taking a Cold War, bipolar approach to the world, where proxy states are defended by proxy armies and attacked by proxy guerillas. In such a scenario, you know exactly who you are arming and why. That basically describes a recent *New York Times* headline, proclaiming a "proxy war" in Syria between the U.S. and Russia.

Russia, on the other hand, has moved on to a post-Cold War, multipolar view of the world, in which the superpower vs. superpower struggle has been replaced by a civilizational battle with radical Islam. Russia sees a very real risk that the radical Islamist teachings of ISIS will be exported back to Russian soil, leading to a surge of terrorist activity in places such as the North Caucasus and the radicalization of the Russian Muslim population. By some estimates, there are now 1,700 Russians fighting on the side of ISIS in Syria and northern Iraq.

Of the two views of the world, the first is far more comforting, even if it's very wrong, because it means that the U.S. does not need to change its stance vis-à-vis Russia. It can continue with its Cold War mentality, its bloc thinking, its export of democracy to war-torn regions, and the support of guerilla groups even if they offer no hope for future governmental stability.

The second is far more challenging, because it means that the U.S. foreign policy establishment fundamentally misread what's happening in Libya, in Iraq, in Iran and in Syria. It means that the Arab Spring was not a massive outpouring of support for democracy, but rather, a massive unleashing of new Islamist political actors with their own radical goals for the region.

From this perspective, "disinformation" is not so much information that's wrong, but information that's meant to counter other information. It's not propaganda so much as it is a secondary market for information.

For people who came of age during the Internet era, one of the great maxims for technologists, attributed to Stewart Brand at the first Hackers Conference in 1984, has always been, "Information wants to be free." Judging from what's happening in Syria and Ukraine, it's possible to add a second corollary – "And so does disinformation, because it's so valuable."

Putinology

"I once heard a very good explanation from a very wise person about why we will never be able to explain ourselves completely in such a way that everyone will like us. This wise person said, 'Do you know when everyone will love us and cease to criticize us and so on, including criticizing us for no reason?'

And I asked, 'When?'

And he said, 'When we dissolve our army, when we concede all our natural resources to them as a concession and when we sell all our land to Western investors. That's when they'll cease to criticize us.'"

- Dmitry Peskov, Kremlin spokesperson, *Kommersant* interview, February 2014

Putinologists vs. Kremlinologists

During the Cold War, the fashionable term for Russia foreign policy experts was "Kremlinologists." The basic idea, of course, was that knowing what happened inside the Kremlin was the single best guide to what was happening in Soviet society. As a result, Kremlinologists rigorously studied photos of Victory Day parades on Red Square to see who was in favor, and who wasn't. They analyzed official Communist Party speeches – as presented by state-controlled propaganda such as Pravda – for clues as to future foreign policy moves.

The only problem is that Kremlinologists failed. Not only failed, but failed miserably. In "The Signal and the Noise," his book on data and forecasting, statistician and political data-cruncher Nate Silver called out the 1990s-era Kremlinologists as possibly the worst possible forecasters in any field, ever. Despite claiming to be experts with a pulse on the Kremlin, they failed to predict one of the biggest calamities in the history of the 20th century - the breakup of the Soviet Union.

And the danger now is that the new generation of Kremlinologists – call them Putinologists – are at risk of failing in the same way. Once again, the nation's best Russia analysts are single-mindedly focused on a solitary individual – Vladimir Putin – and what his plans are for Russia. They are so focused on Putin that they have lost sight of other broad developments taking place within Russian society, or other emerging sources of power within the Kremlin.

It's not only the breathless spate of articles (both scholarly and non-scholarly) proclaiming to know what the Russian leader thinks – it's the remarkable amount of pulp nonfiction that's been created around Vladimir Putin. Ben Judah's fictional accounting of what Putin may or may not be thinking in summer 2014 – "Behind the Scenes in Putin's Court: The Private Life of a Latter-Day Dictator" - stands out. It portrays Putin as a tsar-like figure surrounded by a quiet hush of courtiers and loyal sycophants, obsessed with the history of other Russian tsars.

The tsar motif is a popular one, to be sure, when describing Vladimir. No wonder Judah made sure to mention that Vladimir Putin was a fan of Ivan the Terrible, Peter the Great, and Catherine the Great – and that he was particularly struck by a recent Russian fictional work, "The Third Empire," about an imaginary Vladimir II, "the in-gatherer of all Russian lands."

The latest entrant in the Putinology game is "The New Tsar" by former *New York Times* Moscow bureau chief Steven Lee Myers, which rehashes a number of well-known anecdotes about Putin's early life, filling in the years from 2000-2015 with all of the tragedies that have befallen Russia over the years – the sinking of the Kursk, the Chechen Wars, the Ukraine crisis. In doing so, the book hopes to "explain in full-bodied, almost Shakespearian fashion why he acts the way he does. Putin's regime, Myers suggests, has been a 15-year Shakespearian tragedy.

And before "The New Tsar," there were plenty of entrants from high-profile Russia watchers. There's "The Man Without a Face" from Masha Gessen, which portrays Putin as a sinister KGB operative with very little morality. And there's "Putin's

Kleptocracy" by Karen Dawisha, which portrays Putin as the evil CEO-like figure of a giant, corrupt empire.

Those three motifs – Putin as tsar, Putin as corrupt CEO and Putin as crafty KGB agent – are easily the most popular. The problem, however, is that these motifs are basically turning the study of Vladimir Putin into a game of Google Auto-Complete.

Type in "Vladimir Putin is" within the Google search box, and what do you get? "Putin is bored." "Putin is dead." "Putin is evil." "Putin is powerful." Plug all four of those Google Auto-Complete answers into a piece about Vladimir Putin, and the piece basically writes itself. It's easy to create a cartoon caricature of Putin. He's evil, he's powerful, he's a despot and he's bored.

And, so by resorting to these cartoon caricatures of Putin, Putinologists are almost certain to miss what is really happening in the modern Russia. Take the new book by Steven Lee Myers, for example, which was informed by nearly a decade of covering Russia for the *New York Times* in Moscow.

The book portrays the Kremlin as an impenetrable house of doom, a place where evil plots are hatched – to silence dissidents, to start wars, to snatch assets away from oligarchs and to spend the nation's wealth recklessly on vanity projects. By focusing so much on Putin, however, the book leaves half the picture unfinished.

This is an important point, and symptomatic of what former Kremlin insider Gleb Pavlovsky described in an August 2015 op-ed written by Ivan Krastev for the *New York Times*, "What the West Gets Wrong About Russia." Pavlovsky takes to task the "myriad memos and papers struggling to understand the mindset driving Russia's strategic behavior" through the prism of just a single individual.

Instead, as Pavlovsky explains, "Kremlin policy is fashioned rather like the music of a jazz group; its continuing improvisation is an attempt to survive the latest crisis." In other words, we are missing the inner complexity of what's happening inside the Kremlin by turning everyone into an amateur Putinologist. What's happening in Putin's Russia is not a Shakespearian tragedy –it's the improvisation of a complex jazz song.

Just as during the Cold War, it may mean that Kremlinologists miss the massive, wholesale changes taking place in the modern Russia. They may miss changes happening within the ruling United Russia party, the infighting between different political clans, and the rise of the new ideologists responsible for the "end of the world" mentality taking hold in the Kremlin.

These same Putinologists, for example, completely missed Russian military aggression in Ukraine – despite Putin warning them nearly a decade ago about continued NATO encroachment to Russian borders. They missed Russia's military intervention in Syria.

So what are we missing now?

Putin, godfather of the Russian state

As part of this geopolitical conspiracy narrative involving Russia, the tendency in the Western media is to portray Russian President Vladimir Putin as the unchallenged authoritarian leader of a vast kleptocratic state held together by a "vertical of power" that unites the Kremlin, the military, the FSB and the various state organs responsible for law and order in Russia.

The "vertical of power" metaphor has become so ingrained, that most people believe that power travels up to Putin and down from Putin almost effortlessly thanks to his manipulation of the military, law enforcement and the media. The mechanism for this is typically referred to as "the authorities" - a favorite Russian word that can be used to describe just about anything, but usually implies a source of unchallenged power.

However, what if Putin's "vertical of power" is actually "horizontal"?

A more nuanced view of Kremlin power politics would recognize how Putin has managed to corral the various competing blocs and clans around him – the "siloviki," the energy sector heads, the military heads, the economic liberals, and the "systemic opposition" into one big happy coalition. Instead of one long "vertical" that stretches from the Kremlin down to local grassroots law enforcement officials, it's really much more of a vast, intertwined network.

Russian political consultant Evgeny Minchenko has actually created a sophisticated chart to show the vast, inter-locking relationships of those who appear to have Putin's ear. According to him, "Politburo 2.0" is "an informal network structure for interests reconciliation of elite clans, in which Vladimir Putin is the main arbitrator and the most influential figure."

And it's not just Minchenko who sees a different type of power structure at work in Russia. University of Central London scholar Alena Ledeneva refers to power in Russia as the "Sistema" – an informal network of alliances, verbal agreements and an uncodified code of behavior that's essential for getting anything done in Russia. The Russian state is so bogged down with bureaucracy and entrenched corruption, that the only way to get things to work is through this informal "sistema."

Viewing the Kremlin as a "system" of power rather than a "vertical" of power would have huge implications for Western foreign policy. For one, it would imply that simply leaning on Putin and his inner circle might not be enough – if the generals and spooks and freelance nationalists are off on their own and not completely under his control, he may not be able to rein them in when it comes time to wind down the Ukraine adventure.

And the existence of this "network of power" might explain something like the audacious Boris Nemtsov murder, which took place just steps away from the Kremlin. If you view Putin as the unchallenged authoritarian leader of the country, then the only possible conclusion is that Putin "signed off" on the contract murder.

However, if you recognize the existence of rival clans and coalitions, then it's possible that any of these rivals – most notably the rabid nationalists pushing for more aggressive military action in Ukraine or the Chechen warlord contingent led by Ramzan Kadyrov – could have ordered the murder as a way to set up Putin.

Much has been made of Putin's inner circle and how he has managed to enrich them to the tune of billions of dollars, while simultaneously making billions for himself in the process. The key, of course, is being able to dole out favors to people – stakes in a company, the governorship of a region, economic incentives or a new pipeline deal – in exchange for uncompromising loyalty.

Nowhere is this better seen than in the weekly news shots on Russian state-run TV of Putin holding court with his loyal ministers and regional heads. As Peter Pomerantsev pointed out his wonderfully entertaining book on Russian propaganda, "Nothing is True and Everything is Possible," the TV sessions bear an uncanny resemblance to the scene from *The Godfather*, in which Marlon Brando gathers his various mafia dons:

"There's a little scene that gets played out on the Ostankino channels every week. The president sits at the head of a long table. Along each side sit the governors of every region: the western, central, northeastern, and so on. The president points to each one, who tells him what's going on in his patch. "Rogue terrorists, pensions unpaid, fuel shortages. ..." The governors looked petrified. The president toys with them... "Well, if you can't sort out the mess in your backyard, we can always find a different governor..."

Pomerantsev continues:

For a long time, I couldn't remember what the scene reminded me of. Then I realized: it's straight out of *The Godfather*, when Marlon Brando gathers the mafia bosses from the five boroughs. Quentin

Tarantino used a similar scene when Lucy Liu meets with the heads of the Tokyo Yakuza clans in *Kill Bill* – it's a mafia movie trope. And it fits the image the Kremlin has for the President..."

The veiled threat, of course, is that everything that has been doled out can be quickly reclaimed. The classic example, of course, is Putin's relationship with disgraced Russian billionaire oil oligarch Mikhail Khodorkovsky. Once one of Russia's most powerful business leaders, Khodorkovsky went too far, in Putin's opinion. He sought to challenge Putin personally. That left Putin one option – to go after his ill-gotten oil stakes – and then, eventually, to strip him of everything and ship him away to prison in Siberia on trumped-up charges.

There are many more examples. Suffice it to watch a YouTube clip where Putin humbles a billionaire oligarch, Oleg Deripaska, on national TV in 2009. After a few choice words from Putin, Deripaska walks over to Putin, apologizes, signs a piece of paper, and that's it.

Karen Dawisha calls this a "kleptocracy," while some Western think tanks describe Putin as the "CEO of Russia" or the head of "Russia, Inc." Either way, Putin is seen as the ultimate arbiter and mafia godfather, determining which way the spoils of the state should flow.

Even the term used by Russians to describe the people in power – "the authorities" – actually has overtones from the criminal underworld, where the "authority" is the highest-ranking criminal official. No wonder Putin so often drops prison slang into his addresses – the most notable being his use of "We'll rub them out in the outhouse" - to describe his Chechen anti-terrorist campaign back in 1999.

As a result, one of the key motivations of Western sanctions was to put pressure on the people closest to Putin. The logic was simple: if these people start to complain, they will put pressure on Putin, who will eventually relent. That might happen – or might not.

As we've seen already, it may be the case that people who complain loudly enough are simply jettisoned from Putin's inner circle – witness the example of Vladimir Yakunin, the former head of Russian Railways who was once one of Putin's most trusted insiders. And now there's talk about the "cleansing of the Russian elite." The implication is clear: if you're not with Putin, then you're against him, and the state will find a way to extend its long arm to reach out and take everything from you.

It's easy, then, to view Putin as the godfather of a vast criminal state. That's certainly been the tactics of the Russian opposition, which has focused on the unheard-of graft and corruption within the bureaucracy. All of it, they say, points to the broader thesis that Putin's inner circle has enriched itself while the rest of the nation suffers. Take the example of Peskov's watch – a funny Internet meme that focused on a $500,000 watch that showed up on the wrist of Kremlin spokesperson at his wedding.

But in embracing this narrative, we may be setting ourselves up for the same kinds of mistakes that Kremlinologists made during the Cold War, in which they carefully scrutinized the Victory Day parades on Moscow's Red Square for any signs of who's in favor, who's not. But what these Kremlinologists missed entirely was the bigger picture – the slow, steady dissolve of the Soviet Union itself.

By just watching carefully choreographed Kremlin news clips (some of them replayed days later just for fun when Putin happens to be missing from the Kremlin), we may be missing all the palace intrigues and loose network of clans, coalitions and factions that make up any traditional power network. The Kremlin may portray itself as an impregnable fortress with officials marching in lockstep with Putin, but it doesn't mean this matches up with the reality of what's happening inside.

The leadership secrets of Vladimir the Great

If you take the metaphor of Vladimir Putin as the "CEO of Russia, Inc." seriously, then it's hard not to ignore quite a few practical leadership lessons on how Putin has managed to tame such an unruly state. To get all the rival clans and competing power interests to march in lockstep, he's reinvented himself as a modern-day tsar – but a tsar with an MBA.

Flash back 25 years ago during the waning days of the Cold War, when Wess Roberts published the wonderfully entertaining "Leadership Secrets of Attila the Hun." So why not a similar study of the leadership secrets of Vladimir Vladimirovich Putin? (Or, if you prefer, "Tsar Vladimir" or "Vladimir the Great"?)

At the time, of course, "Attila the Hun" read almost as an irreverent take on business management books of the era, a post-modernist Machiavelli for the MBA set. Back in 1990, in a business world used to the practical advice of Peter Drucker and Tom Peters and very serious dissertations about management and business – the idea that you could make up an entire life history of one of the world's foremost historical figures and, moreover, actually turn it into a bestselling management book was inspired, to say the least.

After all, the book on Attila the Hun apparently inspired H. Ross Perot, who wrote about the book in his history of GM, and it went on to become a bestseller. For H. Ross Perot, the idea that someone like Genghis Khan might have insights into the world of guerilla marketing didn't seem so absurd after all.

In a similar way, Vladimir Putin is a historical figure who probably has a lot to tell and has been widely misunderstood, But telling his story needs to be done in a way that is fun, entertaining and perhaps just a little bit post-modernist. (And if it could somehow include GIFs and parody Twitter accounts, then all the better.)

While there have been several different Western works published about Putin – the ones by Ben Judah ("Fragile Empire: How Russia Fell In and Out of Love with Vladimir Putin"), Masha Gessen ("The Man Without a Face: The Unlikely Rise of Vladimir Putin") and Fiona Hill and Clifford Gaddy ("Mr. Putin: Operative in the Kremlin") stand out as three of the best – they have essentially re-hashed anecdotes from Putin's earlier era, snippets from the only officially authorized autobiography about Putin ("First Person," released in 2000), and hearsay from insiders close to the Kremlin's inner circle.

Even one of the most entertaining stories about Putin's daily routine – Ben Judah's piece for Newsweek ("Behind the Scenes in Putin's Court") in August 2014 – was largely assembled from hearsay and rumors and constructed from conversations with people who declined to give their names. It read as more the work of fiction and speculation than a real, behind-the-scenes look at Vladimir Putin. We learned that Putin likes to go for a 2-hour swim, that he disdains the Internet but loves the popular Moscow tabloids, and keeps his most loyal insiders in a state of permanent agitation as they seek to fulfill his every whim.

In Russia, the idea of publishing an unauthorized biography is challenging at best, so such a book on the leadership secrets of Putin probably wouldn't be possible without the official blessing of the Kremlin. Unofficially, Russian press cannot write about Putin's private life, including his divorce or his children. Thus, what is known about Putin is what Putin chooses to tell us about himself.

Putin is often portrayed as cold and unsmiling – and yet, that very absence of a smile entices us, the way the smile of the Mona Lisa has been endless dissected for centuries. When we see him hugging a koala at the G8 Summit in Australia in 2014 or sulking after not being invited to a dinner, it is almost as if we are seeing an entirely different person than the one the Western media has shown us.

At a time when Cold War tensions have become so intensely personal, and when Vladimir Putin seems to personify Western views of Russia, it is taking a closer look at what makes him tick – and to see if those insights might have broader insights for others.

On the surface, of course, selecting Vladimir Putin as a leadership figure seems faintly fantastical. In the West, he is viewed more often as a dictator, a strongman, the head of a kleptocracy, a mafia leader, a throwback to the Soviet era, and an authoritarian, no-nonsense guy who enjoys riding around on horses without a shirt.

But take a step back.

Putin is routinely listed as among the most influential figures in modern world history, the most powerful man on the planet, and the leader of a disgraced former superpower that now makes world headlines with just about everything he does.

By some estimates, his personal net worth is more than $40 billion, making him a worthy template for anyone attempting to build a corporate fortune from scratch. He's managed to stay in power for fifteen years despite an unpopular war in Chechnya, a financial crisis, and now an epic standoff with the West that briefly sent the Russian economy into a tailspin.

Women – from French and Italian politicians to Russian Olympic gymnasts - swoon over him. A disappearance from Russian airwaves for more than a few days is enough to set off mass panic and speculation as to his potential whereabouts.

Clearly, he's doing something right.

In Russia, in fact, Putin's approval ratings are off the charts. After the annexation of Crimea, state-run opinion polls estimated his approval ratings in the mid-to-higher 80s. Almost unanimously, his pronouncements on state airwaves are taken to be gospel, and his camera-ready appearance is reassuring to a populace that experienced the chaos of the Yeltsin era, the disappointments of the Gorbachev era, and the long, slow stagnation under Brezhnev during the twilight of the Soviet era.

Putin's hands-on management style, his ability to control competing clans and rivals, and his willingness to stake his reputation on a single vision – Russia as a great power again, feared by the West and revered by emerging nations looking to transition to a multipolar world order- have made him a crowd favorite.

And it's not just in the West where Putin has emerged as am intriguing figure. A biography in China about Putin published in 2014 was a runaway bestseller.

And, in the West, simply putting Putin on the cover of a major news or business magazine is enough to ensure mass readership. *TIME*, *The Economist*, *Business Week* and *Newsweek* are among the magazines that routinely put Putin on the cover. *TIME* has named Putin "Person of the Year," and he routinely shows up in *Forbes'* listing of the world's most powerful people.

One thing is clear – a key to Putin's success over the past 15 years has been his ability to craft a coherent worldview and post-Soviet ideology for the Russian people. Is that really any different from crafting a coherent long-term strategy for one of the world's most powerful multinationals?

The strange symbiotic relationship between Vladimir Putin and Donald Trump

Russia and America may be more alike than you think, judging by their strange infatuation with testosterone-fuelled, no-holds-barred political leaders. In America, one year ahead of the 2016 presidential election, the Republican frontrunner is still Donald Trump; in Russia, Vladimir Putin's popularity continues to skyrocket faster than Russia's SS-N-30 Kalibr missiles cruising through Syrian airspace.

But the relationship goes deeper than that. Trump needs Putin in 2016, and Putin needs Trump in 2016. It's a deeply symbiotic relationship.

It's Donald Trump who's now pointing to Vladimir Putin's military tactics in Syria shows as proof of why America is so weak in the world and why it's necessary to engage – rather than isolate - Russia. And it's Vladimir Putin who's now suggesting that Donald Trump might be the only American presidential candidate in 2016 with whom he might be able to work once Obama's gone.

It's gotten to the point that even Russian state-owned media (or, as they prefer to call it in the West, state-owned propaganda) is actively promoting Trump's political commentary about the mess in Iraq and Libya as proof that Putin's policies are the right approach in tackling ISIS in Syria. According to Trump's logic, the Middle East would actually be safer with Hussein, Gaddafi and a stronger Assad – and that helps Putin in making his case to the world.

The U.S. media, too, is using the figure of Vladimir Putin and the Russian military intervention in Syria as a way to differentiate between the presidential candidates. At the first Democratic debate in mid-October 2015, it was the question of what to do with Vladimir Putin that was used to differentiate between the foreign policy approaches of the respective candidates.

As a result, U.S. politicians who once used the figure of Vladimir Putin to take down Obama are now using the figure of Putin to take down Donald Trump or Hillary Clinton. It makes for good politics and even better theater.

Appearing on NBC's "Tonight Show" with Jimmy Fallon, it was Republican candidate Carly Fiorina who suggested that Trump and Putin "have a lot in common." The innuendo, of course, was that Putin is a repugnant figure; therefore Trump is a repugnant figure. In short, Putin is a "foil character" for any U.S. politician, enabling him or her to define who they are by what Putin is.

What will be interesting, of course, is to monitor how the Putin-Trump relationship plays out over the long haul of the 2016 U.S. presidential campaign. Trump has been the only Republican candidate who says he'd be able to work with Putin – everyone else has said they'd isolate Putin even further, or mount their own military efforts to counter Putin's aggressive moves.

So, in the upside down world of U.S. presidential politics, Vladimir Putin has actually emerged as one of the most important wildcard factors. He has the ability to determine the way both Republicans and Democrats view U.S. foreign policy.

For the Republicans, he's a "foil character" to separate the Republican contenders from Hillary Clinton and Barack Obama.

For the Democrats, he's a scary Russian version of Donald Trump – a worst nightmare of what might happen if a hawkish Republican is installed in the Oval Office with a finger on the nuclear button.

And that means the harder Putin pushes in Ukraine and Syria, the worse it is for Hillary Clinton, who famously backed the reset with Russia (something she obviously regrets these days). And it also means that the more missiles fall in Syria, the more the Republican contenders are going to push for a muscular foreign policy vision.

That leaves just one person in America capable of dealing with Vladimir Putin – Donald Trump.

The reason is clear. On the surface, Putin and Trump have a lot in common, beyond just the testosterone factor. They're both used to blustering on the world stage. They're both not afraid to say what they think. And they both talk about making their nation great again.

One of the more interesting academic studies of Vladimir Putin ("Sex, Politics and Putin") is from Clark University professor Valerie Sperling, who basically took a gender-based approach to analyzing Putin and why he's so popular in Russia. What she found is that the Russian people are predisposed to picking leaders that embody the same "macho" traits found in Vladimir Putin.

As a result, writes Sperling, "A masculine image of the Russian president has been intentionally created by the Kremlin's image makers and then actively promoted through numerous macho acts, such as fishing and riding bare-chested, showing off his martial arts skills, and using foul language and criminal underworld slang."

In other words, if it weren't Vladimir Putin who took over Russia in 2000, it would have been someone like him – perhaps even someone more aggressive and militaristic. That's an argument that's been made before, with Thomas Graham of Kissinger Associates suggesting in August 2014 that America's beef isn't so much with Putin, it's with Russia itself. Graham writes:

"Putin is the dominant figure in Russia today, and he makes the final decisions on foreign policy. But we need to remember that he operates in a political context and does not have a free hand, as he must balance the competing factions around him to maintain his own position. Moreover, he is a product of the Russian elite, and he gives voice to its consensus on Russia's role in the world, which has deep roots in history and strategic tradition. His departure might lead to a change in style, but it will have little impact on the substance of Russian foreign policy. In short, we have a Russia problem, not a Putin problem."

Framing the U.S.-Russia relationship as a Russia problem and not a Putin problem matters. It serves to underscore the similarities between Trump and Putin rather than their differences. Culture and national identity matter, but not in the way we think: Putin is not a purely Russian phenomenon and Trump – with his capitalist swagger - is not a purely American phenomenon.

As David Ignatius of the *Washington Post* argued in an op-ed in August 2015:

"Donald Trump is in some respects an American version of Putin. Like the Russian leader, he seeks to reverse his country's losses and return its former glory. He promises a restoration of power and prestige without trifling about the details."

This point is worth taking into deeper consideration by the U.S. foreign policy establishment. The current Western narrative is that Putin is impossible to deal with, that his worldview is not worth listening to, and that his macho aggressive posturing is going to continue to get Russia into trouble, first in Ukraine and now in Syria.

But what if Trump and Putin are really part and parcel of the same political phenomenon? In both the U.S. and Russia, we may be observing what happens when the populations of two former superpowers search for a bold leader who will restore a complex, multipolar world to the way it was before the end of the Cold War. Just as the U.S. political establishment can no longer ignore Donald Trump, the U.S. foreign policy establishment can no longer ignore Vladimir Putin.

The 10 most important lines from Vladimir Putin's 2015 UN speech

It's in his public speeches and appearances on Russian state-owned TV that we can learn the most about Russian President Vladimir Putin's worldview. A few events stand out for their ability to define this worldview, including his now famous speech delivered at the Munich Security Conference in 2007, which largely foreshadowed much of the aggressive posturing we are now seeing in Russian foreign policy.

Vladimir Putin's much anticipated speech at the 70th anniversary session of the UN General Assembly in September 2015 may not have been another Munich, but it certainly came close. In his speech, he referenced many of the same themes – especially the perils of a unipolar world ruled by a single sovereign superpower – that he mentioned in his infamous 2007 speech.

With the world celebrating the 70th anniversary of the defeat of Nazi Germany in 2015, Putin used his UN speech to outline in broad strokes his vision for a modern version of a grand "anti-Hitler coalition" led by the UN to defeat ISIS (and prop up Syria's "valiant" fighters) in the Middle East.

The Russian leader also threw his support behind international law (or, at least, Russia's interpretation of international law), the central role of the UN in preserving global security, and the need to avoid double standards in international relations.

The following are some of the most powerful quotes from Putin's UN speech, showing how he views the world and illustrating why the U.S. and Russia remain at ideological loggerheads over so many issues.

On the evils of a superpower hegemon:

"We all know that after the end of the Cold War — everyone is aware of that — a single center of domination emerged in the world, and then those who found themselves at the top of the pyramid were tempted to think that if they were strong and exceptional, they knew better and they did not have to reckon with the U.N..."

In one fell swoop, Putin goes after "American exceptionalism" and the problems created by a unipolar world in which there is only one sovereign superpower. Putin has long advocated for a multipolar world in which the power of the United States to determine the rules of the game would be curtailed.

On the need to form a new coalition against ISIS:

"But I remind you that the key decisions on the principles guiding the cooperation among states, as well as on the establishment of the United Nations, were made in our country, in Yalta, at the meeting of the anti-Hitler coalition leaders."

This is the reference to World War II that everyone expected from Putin, given the historically significant 70th anniversary date. But he also throws in a reference to Yalta as a reminder that Russia has been at the forefront of determining the world's security architecture for 70 years. (Moreover, referencing Yalta—located in Crimea—carries its own form of special significance for Russia.) The reference to the "anti-Hitler coalition" reminds everyone of the sacrifices Russia suffered in the war, while simultaneously presenting ISIS as a similar type of great evil in the world.

On the danger of color revolutions:

"We also remember certain episodes from the history of the Soviet Union. Social experiments for export, attempts to push for changes within other countries based on ideological preferences, often led to tragic consequences and to degradation rather than progress... It seemed, however, that far from learning from others' mistakes, everyone just keeps repeating them, and so the export of revolutions, this time of so-called democratic ones, continues..."

This is actually a bold attempt to equate the Soviet Union's use of Communist ideology to achieve geopolitical aims with America's use of liberal-democratic ideology to achieve similar aims. Both ideologies are dangerous, Putin warns. Moreover, the "export of revolutions" theme fits right in with Russia's fear of "color revolutions" and "democracy promotion." Rather than bringing democracy, these "exports" only bring disaster and human suffering.

On the dangers of a unipolar world:

"I cannot help asking those who have caused the situation, do you realize now what you've done? But I am afraid no one is going to answer that. Indeed, policies based on self-conceit and belief in one's exceptionality and impunity have never been abandoned."

In one question – "Do you realize now what you've done?" – Putin seeks to belittle the Obama administration for its weakness and naïveté on foreign policy as well as once again take America to task for its "exceptionalism." This single line became the title of the RT video of Putin's UN speech, and it obviously has a lot of appeal for future propaganda purposes.

On the reasons for the Ukraine crisis:

"First, they continue their policy of expanding NATO. What for? If the Warsaw Bloc stopped its existence, the Soviet Union collapsed and, nevertheless, the NATO continues expanding as well as its military infrastructure. Then they offered the poor Soviet countries a false choice: either to be with the West or with the East. Sooner or later, this logic of confrontation was bound to spark off a grave geopolitical crisis. This is exactly what happened in Ukraine, where the discontent of population with the current authorities was used and the military coup was orchestrated from outside — that triggered a civil war as a result."

Putin once again reiterates the Kremlin's logic for the Ukraine crisis, showing that the crisis flowed naturally from NATO expansion eastward after the end of the Cold War and continued attempts to encroach on Russia's historical sphere of influence. The events in Ukraine were nothing less than a coup d'état organized by external actors, and the situation now is a "civil war" rather than military aggression by Russia.

On the true meaning of Russia's actions in Syria:

"However, it's not about Russia's ambitions, dear colleagues, but about the recognition of the fact that we can no longer tolerate the current state of affairs in the world. What we actually propose is to be guided by common values and common interests, rather than ambitions."

Once again, Putin links Russia to Europe and a common shared history and common shared values. He makes it clear that Russia's geopolitical ambitions have been exaggerated by the West and that Russia is ready for action in the Middle East, even if the West isn't.

On the need to avoid double standards in international relations:

"Every term in international law and international affairs should be clear, transparent and have uniformly understood criteria. We are all different, and we should respect that. No one has to conform to a single development model that someone has once and for all recognized as the only right one."

This is Putin's attempt fight back against what Russia perceives to be a "double standard" in the international arena. He again references the U.S. with the term "single development model" (without actually naming the U.S.) in an attempt to appeal to all the non-Western leaders at the UN who feel that the U.S. has too powerful of a role in global affairs.

On the rightful role of the UN:

"Russia believes in the huge potential of the United Nations, which should help us avoid a new global confrontation and engage in strategic cooperation. Together with other countries, we will consistently work towards strengthening the central coordinating role of the U.N."

Russia plays up the "central coordinating role" of the UN mostly to ensure that its unique veto privilege within the UN Security Council gives it an automatic trump card against any Western initiatives to punish it further. (Just remember how hard Russia lashed back at the West when there were hints that certain nations would try to strip Russia of its UN veto power after the MH17 tragedy.) Putin also tries to position Russia as a believer in international norms, as a great power with a great role to play in the world.

On Russia's economic integration projects:

"Contrary to the policy of exclusiveness, Russia proposes harmonizing original economic projects. I refer to the so-called integration of integrations based on universal and transparent rules of international trade. As an example, I would like to cite our plans to interconnect the Eurasian economic union, and China's initiative of the Silk Road economic belt."

The "integration of integrations" line was mocked on Twitter, but it shows how Russia is trying to position itself as the "integrator" between Europe and Asia. Putin also serves a wakeup call that the Eurasian Economic Union is not an attempt to reconstitute the Soviet Union – it's an attempt to build economic bridges with its geopolitical neighbors. Here, he also references Russia's pivot to China, which is positioned as a purely economic strategy rather than a ploy to weaken American power in Asia.

On the unintended consequences of Western foreign policy:

"It would be equally irresponsible to try to manipulate extremist groups and place them at one's service in order to achieve one's own political goals in the hope of later dealing with them or, in other words, liquidating them. To those who do so, I would like to say — dear sirs, no doubt you are dealing with rough and cruel people, but they're in no way primitive or silly. They are just as clever as you are, and you never know who is manipulating whom."

Again, Putin hits back at the Obama administration's naïveté in dealing with ISIS and his unwillingness to go after the terrorists directly. He also mocks Obama for his belief that a "moderate opposition" is possible in the Middle East.

While Putin's remarks may not have gone over so well in the U.S., it's worth remembering the intro to Putin's Munich speech: "And if my comments seem unduly polemical, pointed or inexact to our colleagues, then I would ask you not to get angry with me. After all, this is only a conference." It certainly made for some colorful theater at the UN.

The House of Putin vs. The House of Saud

The West's double standards in international relations have become a cornerstone of Russia's approach to foreign policy. The theme appears again and again in the speeches of Russian President Vladimir Putin and the commentary from the Russian Foreign Ministry, even before Putin's UN speech in 2015.

And nowhere are these "double standards" more visible than in the Middle East, where Russian foreign policy has taken a distinctly anti-American tack, chiding the U.S. for its role in fomenting instability in Iraq, Libya and Syria.

Take, for example, the recent U.S.-backed Saudi military intervention in Yemen against Iranian-backed proxies. The following hypothetical summary could just as easily describe Russia's intervention in Ukraine against what it perceives to be NATO and U.S.-backed proxies:

"An oil-rich regional power, feeling threatened by an armed coup near its border as well as the appearance of a rival in its historical sphere of influence, reacts quickly and decisively. This regional power amasses more than 100,000 troops and intervenes militarily in a nation without formal support from the UN or any other international security body. This same regional power attempts to restore the deposed leader of the armed coup, again without international support. As a result, a localized civil war threatens to become a regional war and the basis for a global proxy war that could last decades."

It's immediately clear how these double standards impact the global order.

In one case, Saudi Arabia is a long-time partner of the United States and essentially gets a "pass" to do whatever needs to be done, no questions asked. In the other case, Russia is a long-time rival of the United States and gets a firm economic shakedown for its efforts to assert order and stability in Ukraine.

No wonder Russia's Ministry of Foreign Affairs and Foreign Minister Sergey Lavrov were so distressed by what they saw as America's "double standards" for the House of Putin and the House of Saud. As Foreign Minister Lavrov pointed out on March 27, 2015: "I have no choice but to use this hackneyed cliché: Obvious double standards have been applied. Certainly, we did not want the events that are happening today in Ukraine and Yemen."

But this is more than just the classic case of "Whataboutism" involving Russia that we've seen time and time again. Russia can talk endlessly about the unification of West and East Germany, Argentina's rights to the Falklands, NATO's intervention in Kosovo or Chechnya's right to arm Mexico — and nobody is going to listen much about double standards. Nobody much takes seriously any argument that starts "What about..."

But the case of the House of Saud and the House of Putin shows better than any previous example the way "double standards" at play in the global order are changing the thinking of key Western partners.

If tensions in the Arabian Peninsula persist, they could lead to a re-thinking of the global security order. Nobody much believes in a Fukuyama-like "End of History" thesis anymore, in which liberal capitalist democracies reign supreme in the world, and now it's time to find a new thesis.

And this new thesis has got to include the legitimate interests of the world's growing economic powers — including Russia — as well as serious thinking of how to deal with changing world order where trade blocs are shifting, globalization is halting, and signs of a New Cold War are all around us.

Where all this could play out first is in the Middle East, where the House of Putin and the House of Said have already shown signs of a massive falling-out – and the situation in Syria is not going to help. As if Saudi Arabia's refusal to cut back oil production at OPEC in 2014 wasn't enough to get Russia's attention, there's now the delicate matter of what Saudi Arabia thinks about Russia's growing influence in Iran, Syria and Egypt. This all came to a head in late March 2015, in the form of a Saudi rebuke to Russian President Vladimir Putin, accusing him and Russia of "hypocrisy" for their role in Syria.

But if the global order is indeed changing, and Saudi Arabia feels confident in its role as the regional hegemon, then the old days of the Western petrodollar system propping up a conservative (even authoritarian) regime in Saudi Arabia could be coming to an end.

While the West is standing by for now in Yemen, careful not to disrupt global oil supplies in the region, there is a growing feeling in foreign policy circles that the drama of the West's "double standards" with Saudi Arabia is coming to a decisive denouement. And, going forward, that could have a huge impact on not just how the West interacts with the House of Saud, but also how it interacts with the House of Putin.

The trial of Vladimir Putin: Crime and punishment

Now that Vladimir Putin has been in power for more than 15 years and Russia is flexing its military prowess on the global stage, it's perhaps not surprising that the number of books claiming to present an insider view of the Russian president is starting to proliferate. The latest entry is "The New Tsar: The Rise and Reign of Vladimir Putin," a 480-word "biography" of Russian President Vladimir Putin from former *New York Times* Moscow bureau chief Steven Lee Myers, published in late September 2015.

The word "biography" is in quotes here because as its not so much a biography as it is a long, step-by-step recounting of all the crimes, missteps and misdemeanors of Putin's "tsarist" regime from 2000-2015. It's not so much a "biography" as it is a provocative call for the West to bring Putin to justice, in the same vein as "The Trial of Henry Kissinger" was an attempt by British journalist Christopher Hitchens to bring Henry Kissinger to justice for war crimes against humanity.

In short, the "biography" is a recipe for regime change. With apologies to Dostoevsky, it is the ultimate "Crime and Punishment."

The title itself – "The New Tsar" - tells you all you need to know. As Myers endeavors to inform readers, Putin is now the unchallenged tsar of Russia, building a regime that's largely corrupt, egocentric and criminalized. Putin himself has become "bronzed" – impervious to the needs of the real Russian people. Anyone who opposes him winds up dead, in prison or exiled abroad. Anyone who supports him winds up fabulously wealthy, protected as part of an exclusive coterie of individuals who are plundering Russia's vast wealth for their own nefarious gains.

There's just one small problem with this "biography" – Steven Lee Myers didn't actually sit down and interview Vladimir Putin. There's mention of a *New York Times* interview with Putin in 2004, but that was more than a decade ago. There's a personal interview by Myers with Vladimir Yakunin, a member of Putin's inner circle, but there doesn't seem to be much in the way of interviews with other Kremlin insiders unless you scour the footnotes. TL;DR

That's a complaint that the *Christian Science Monitor* voiced in its review of the book. *"Why pretend not to have been there?"* is the question that has to be asked, since the book seems to be so devoid of any first-person experiences. Surely, as part of his time in Moscow as a bureau chief of the *New York Times*, Myers had a chance to interview people who might contribute to a biography of Putin, right?

As can be imagined, the book relies heavily on the refuseniks and outcasts who landed up in the West for their side of the story. (Any surprise which way they tilt?) It would be as if the newspaper *Rossiyskaya Gazeta*, which determines "all the news that's fit to print" in Russia just as the *New York Times* does in the United States, set out to write a "biography" of President Obama, but relied on all the Western fringe elements who somehow wound up in Russia with a grudge to avenge.

And the second big problem is that the book is far too linear and formulaic. Every chapter seems to start with some potentially good accomplishment under Putin's rule, but ends only in sadness, tears and corruption. The book builds a case, point-by-point, of how Putin has become "the most popular leader since Stalin the Terrible." Every chapter is bookended by a tragedy (and there have been a lot of them) – the Chechen wars, the Beslan school massacre, the sinking of the Kursk, the Nemtsov assassination, the imprisonment of the oligarchs, the list goes on and on.

Does anything good ever happen in Russia?

In fact, the biography gets pretty depressing, pretty quick. It's a lot more of the recycled rumors and stories about Putin that we've already heard before – including the old story of the cornered rat in a Soviet-era communal apartment that's often dredged up as an explanation of Putin's foreign policy moves. In each new chapter, the figure of Putin gets scarier and scarier. The schoolyard St. Petersburg punk turns into a nondescript East German KGB agent, who morphs into a scheming, rapacious Petersburg government functionary and then a gray, colorless Kremlin functionary hiding the dark secrets of the Yeltsin regime.

According to Myers, Putin then stars to hang out with "post-Soviet money-grubbing politicians" and a whole host of unsavory characters – including a lot of friends from his old KGB and St. Petersburg days. He starts blowing up apartment buildings to start wars, ordering contract hits on his critics, and resorting to dirty election tricks to defeat any rivals. He starts to siphon off enormous wealth and begins building palatial estates, all while divorcing his wife, having plastic surgery and getting his hands dirty with all kinds of shady business dealings.

In the process, Putin transforms into the ultimate "Bond-style villain." This is who Myers wants you to believe Putin is.

What we do find out about Putin's personal life is told largely third-hand, via the Kremlin's propaganda mouthpieces or via unauthorized accounts that have been leaked into the foreign media. (Apparently, there's a juicy work circulating in the German media about Putin's family and another book with gossip about the Kremlin press corps.) We find out that a long expose by Ben Judah on Putin in *Newsweek* in 2014 was actually based on a Russian TV show about Putin.

The entire first piece of the book about Putin's early years and rise in St. Petersburg is lifted almost entirely by a first-person biography penned by Putin himself, together with the help of some journalists vetted by the Kremlin. Other entire sections are lifted from Yeltsin's autobiography. So what is Myers bringing new to the table?

The events in Ukraine and Syria merit little more than two chapters grafted on to the book at the end. By the time you reach page 400 of a 480-page book, it's clear that the cascade of events in Ukraine are only going to merit the rapid-fire staccato of a *New York Times* breaking news lead. Either Myers intended to wrap the book up in 2014 before events in Ukraine broke (and just in time to sabotage the Sochi Olympics), or the current Putinphobia in the media seemed like as good as time as any to push a huge anti-Putin biography.

Yet, it's hard to argue that "The New Tsar" is a mammoth piece of scholarship and it's hard to overlook the number of sources and footnotes. Myers obviously did his homework. And, yet, something sticks in one's craw about the final result. If a biography is really just a call for regime change, shouldn't we really just be calling it propaganda?

Economic War

"Today there are two great peoples on earth who, starting from different points, seem to advance toward the same goal: these are the Russians and the Anglo-Americans... Their point of departure is different, their paths are varied; nonetheless, each one of them seems called by a secret design of Providence to hold in its hands one day the destinies of half the world."

- Alexis de Tocqueville, *Democracy in America* (1835)

Russia needs a new foreign policy paradigm

When it comes to exerting influence in the world, Moscow needs to start thinking in terms of economic, not just military or strategic, spheres of interest. Or, in the words of Russian President Vladimir Putin, there needs to be more focus on the "integration of integrations."

Russia – standing between Europe and Asia – has an opportunity to become a key part of any economic integration process. Russia, which has historically relied on "hard power" – nuclear and conventional military forces – to project power around the globe rather than its ability to broker new trade relationships or create new investment opportunities, needs to re-think its foreign policy paradigm.

The world's top global thinkers appear to agree. At Transformational Trends 2014, a conference co-hosted by *Foreign Policy* and the Policy Planning Staff of the U.S. State Department in Washington, participants agreed on one major transformational trend for the near-term future: States should stop thinking in terms of strategic spheres of interest and start thinking in terms of economic spheres of interest.

And that has huge consequences for Russia. Take, for example, the current situation in Ukraine. At a panel discussion dedicated to "The Changing Nature of the Trans-Atlantic Alliance," the panelists led off with remarks about Ukraine and reflections on why the protestors on Kiev turned their back on Moscow. These young protestors were fighting to join Europe because they wanted the fruits that an expanded economic relationship with the EU promises – jobs, rising incomes and a stable future.

In comparison, Russia appears to be offering goods of only second-degree freshness. The Eurasian Economic Union is a far cry from the European Union. So when initial overtures didn't work as planned, Russia was forced to resort to other forms of leverage – like not so subtle threats about turning off Ukraine's gas.

But that isn't the way the world works anymore. Now, it's all about free trade and robust economic relationships, like the new landmark Transatlantic Trade and Investment Partnership (TTIP) deal that the U.S. is brokering with the EU or the vast new Trans-Pacific Partnership (TPP) deal for Asia-Pacific.

In the words of Hillary Clinton, TTIP is about to create "an economic NATO" and revitalize an alliance that has been at the center of global affairs since the Great Patriotic War. Soon, there will no longer be a clear division between EU and NATO, something that Russia unfortunately realized too late as it saw its traditional allies in the Near Abroad pulled into Europe's orbit.

Other sessions at the Transformational Trends event that in previous years might have turned on traditional notions of foreign policy and diplomacy really came back to key economic issues and the transformative power of trade. A panel on "Rethinking the Greater Middle East," for example, focused on the new types of economic choices that can be presented to a young, social media-savvy generation. In the Arab world, how do you offer the young generation a chance at a good job and bright future so that they don't turn to an ISIS brand of extremism?

That being said, there are signs that Russia an still turn things around, as integration projects like the Eurasian Union and the Customs Union continue to percolate - although it's unclear why any state would prefer to trade with Belarus rather than Germany or Kazakhstan rather than France. Ambassador Miriam Sapiro, Deputy U.S. Trade Representative, applauded Russia for joining the WTO– even if took 18 years.

It will take more than just joining the WTO. Russia needs to offers greater trade and investment potential to its partners in the U.S. and Europe. It's up to Russia to figure out what it can offer the U.S. or Europe if it wants to be treated in the same way as China, a nation viewed by just about everyone as a global economic juggernaut worthy of respect.

Stung by the ongoing impact of economic sanctions and the plummeting price of oil, Russia's leadership seems to recognize that things need to change if the U.S. is ever going to give Russia a central role in its foreign policy calculus.

There is optimism, though, that Russia can turn things around. In its list of the Top 100 Leading Global Thinkers of 2013, *Foreign Policy* magazine specifically tagged Vladimir Putin and Foreign Minister Sergey Lavrov as two of the leading global thinkers in the world right now.

Their inclusion in the list of Top 100 global thinkers was a way of recognizing both of them for searching out new ways to make Russia a leader in global affairs. Russia can no longer rely on energy – and captive energy markets in Europe - if it expects to remain relevant in the world.

Russia should be asking itself some tough questions as it explores ways to expand its relationship with the U.S. and Europe and Asia. How does Russia make itself more relevant to the world's largest economies? As *Foreign Policy* CEO David Rothkopf noted at the event, "This is not your father's foreign policy." He could have just as easily said, "This is not your Cold War-era foreign policy." The new paradigm is economic, not military.

Viewed from this perspective, it's not so much that the U.S. doesn't value a potential strategic relationship with Russia, it's that Russia is no longer perceived as bringing as much to the table as other partners or allies, whether they are in Europe or Asia. To transform the way the world views it, Russia is going to have to transform the way its own leaders view the world.

Forget the reset, it's all about the startup

Due to the lasting Cold War legacy, the focus of U.S.-Russian relations has typically been on foreign policy and diplomacy. However, the good news is that there are actually a growing number of economic linkages between the U.S. and Russian business sectors, both at the grassroots and government level.

These business relations, if allowed to develop further and flourish once sanctions are lifted, could eventually lead to increased trade between the U.S. and Russia, new opportunities for economic cooperation on a global scale, and new partnerships in innovative fields such as IT, software, biotech and clean tech.

The key to this new round of economic cooperation, of course, is finding some way to revive the "reset" policy announced by President Obama and then President Medvedev in 2009. While the "reset" typically referred to a "reset" of diplomatic relations, it also referred to a "reset" in a whole range of other endeavors, including business and innovation.

In 2009, the two nations formed the U.S.-Russia Bilateral Presidential Commission with different working groups for, among other things, re-establishing business links between the two nations and normalizing trade relations. At a time when Russia ranks as one of the largest economies in the world, it still only ranks as America's 28th largest trading partner.

Clearly, there's more that Russia can do to play a greater role in the world economy. According to the U.S.-Russia Bilateral Presidential Commission, WTO accession for Russia was supposed to become a central building block of this economic reintegration policy for Russia. The WTO fits into one of the core ideas of the U.S.-Russia Bilateral Presidential Commission – nations that trade together, stay together.

Inspired by the potential economic benefits of Russia joining the WTO, government leaders in both the U.S. and Russia worked to do all the blocking and tackling required to make the standards, requirements and trade systems of the U.S. and Russia compatible. The short-term goal was to increase the flow of trade and investment to both nations, while the long-term goal was to establish a more stable footing for the U.S. and Russia to hash out their diplomatic differences.

At the same time as government leaders attempted to create a level playing field for businesses (especially export-oriented businesses), Russia was actively working to modernize its economy and move beyond a dependence on a few key commodity exports. The centerpiece of this transformation was Skolkovo, a gleaming new innovation center in Moscow that was essentially created by government fiat as a Russian answer to Silicon Valley.

What started as an incubator and accelerator for high-tech businesses free of the irregularities of Moscow's business sector now includes Skoltech, an innovation and tech school modeled on MIT, as well as the makings of a real innovation ecosystem with VC firms, entrepreneurs and innovation centers.

It is still Russia's hope that this Skolkovo model will be emulated and copied around Russia. Viktor Vekselberg, the head of Skolkovo, has championed the idea that Skolkovo should become an innovation model for Russia's other regions. To put this into practice and overcome the technological losses from economic sanctions, Russia has created a new plan to foster regional economic innovation centers.

This is actually something very new for Russia. In Soviet times, there were "academic cities" of scientists and researchers, but these were typically closed to the West and never became the types of open, high-tech hubs that are now being built all over the world, not just in America. What these Russian regional innovation centers need from the West is not only cash and investment, but also the knowledge of how to commercialize products and attract investors.

Thus far, there are signs that Russia's early attempts to nurture and create an innovation-focused economy are starting to pay dividends. It's cool to be a startup entrepreneur in cities like Moscow -- the city's famed Red October chocolate factory is now a digital media hub and Russian media companies are creating Top 50 lists of tech startups.

Companies like Yandex and Vkontakte are being held up as models of how Russia can create their own homegrown versions of Silicon Valley companies like Google and Facebook. And now innovation has gone beyond just the Internet to include big sectors like biotech and clean tech, both of which are priority areas for the U.S. government. The message should be that Russian companies that have innovative solutions in these areas are welcome in the West.

But there are also discouraging signs that all of this is really a bit of a Potemkin village, meant to dazzle Western guests while simultaneously draining the bank accounts of deep-pocketed investors. You don't build Silicon Valley overnight, and you can't decree the growth of a startup ecosystem using a Five-Year Plan.

And, as Russian venture capital investor Konstantin Fokin noted at the 2013 Russian Innovation Week in Boston, nothing gets done in Russia without the involvement of the government. And that means that anything that's promising or profitable has the risk of being compromised by the state. You need to prove that you can become rich by being a risk-taking entrepreneur. That's easier said than done – you can't import risk-seeking behavior the way you import chicken.

Before U.S.-Russian diplomatic relations deteriorated to their current low point, there were actually a number of top U.S. leaders who put their reputations on the line to make bilateral business cooperation a success. Former U.S. Ambassador to Russia Michael McFaul, for example, attended the 2013 Russian Innovation Week event in Silicon Valley, where he emphasized the strategic importance of the U.S.-Russian business relationship.

Meanwhile, former U.S. Ambassador John Beyrle, who attended the Boston event in 2013, joined the board of the U.S.-Russia Foundation, helping to export American entrepreneurial know-how to Russia. Other business and government leaders are inviting Russian companies to compete for VC money and set up business in their backyard. Still others are inviting leaders to Silicon Valley to see how things work and explore how they can modernize their regional economies.

And, at the Russian Innovation Week 2013 in Boston, one of the surprising stars of the event was none other than the president of Tatarstan, Rustam Minnikhanov, who was invited to keynote alongside Anatoly Chubais and Viktor Vekselberg from the visiting Russian delegation.

Tatarstan, a vibrant economic region located along the Volga, is a symbol of what's possible once the fruits of U.S.-Russian business collaboration are fully distributed across Russia, instead of being concentrated in Moscow, like much of the nation's oil & gas wealth. Just as all happy families are alike, all happy economies are alike. They have strong regional economic hubs that help to diversify a nation's economy. If Tatarstan can become Russia's Austin or Boston or Seattle, then Moscow can retain for itself the role of Russia's Silicon Valley.

Russia should build another Sochi… in Siberia

As Russia shifts its focus from military power to economic power, it's going to open up new investment possibilities within Russia itself, especially in high-value regions such as Russia's Far East and Siberia. At the end of 2013, for example, Russian President Vladimir Putin outlined a vision for the economic development of Siberia. Following through on that type of vision is what Russia needs to wean its economy away from its dependence on oil and gas.

What Russia does best is the type of project of the scale and scope of the $50 billion Sochi Winter Olympics. While it's nice to ruminate on why Russia needs to build a middle-class or encourage the formation of small, entrepreneurial start-ups, that logic seems to fly in the face of the past 300 years of Russian history, in which the state has always taken the leading role in driving growth.

So here's what Russia should do: it should leverage its know-how from the Sochi Winter Olympics to launch another massive, multi-billion project to jump-start economic growth in Siberia.

Quite simply, Russia does big better than it does small. Again and again, Vladimir Putin and his officials emphasized the "gigantic" scale and scope of Sochi 2014. The Sochi Winter Olympics went beyond just constructing brand-new winter sports venues in a city best known as a subtropical beach resort – it included digging holes through mountains to accommodate vast new infrastructure needs and completely re-purposing a low-lying swamp area.

In fact, you could view the "Sochi in Siberia" concept as the third template in the evolving model of massive, large-scale economic development launched in the past five years by Moscow.

The first, of course, was Skolkovo. This was a top-down, state-mandated attempt to create a Silicon Valley in Moscow by government fiat. Sochi was the second template in the model, predicated on building a sports and tourism powerhouse in the south of the country.

A Siberian Sochi would, in a best-case scenario, lead to the creation of a third economic template that could be exported around the nation, from Vladivostok to the Urals. It wouldn't be based around sports and tourism, of course, but around Siberia's vast natural resources.

There are at least three good reasons why Russia should build another Sochi in Siberia.

First of all, Russia desperately needs to attract more investment to its regions. Russia's current economic development model – of attempting to entice Western investors by hosting a series of investment forums around the nation – has started to bear some fruit, but there's always been one big factor mitigating against this: Western investors are scared of losing their money if they do deals with the Russians, especially with sanctions still in place.

From a Western perspective, either you wind up with one of those nasty spats over natural resources, like we've seen over and over again with the oil and gas giants, or you end up with a PR nightmare like you're having right now in Ukraine, where Western investors could see their hard work and efforts dashed by Russia's aggressive posturing on the world stage.

Yet, it's unmistakable that Russia needs to do more to develop its regions, and that Siberia has always represented the natural target for these economic ambitions. Russian President Putin specifically mentioned Siberia in his State of the Nation speech at the end of 2013. Events like the Krasnoyarsk Economic Forum in Siberia make the rational case for development. And ideas from Western think tanks like Brookings continue to percolate in the background.

Just as Sochi was an attempt to boost economic growth along the Black Sea coastline and in the war-torn Caucasus, a Siberian Sochi would attempt to jump-start economic growth in Russia's natural resource-rich hinterland. If Western investors aren't willing to ante up, Russia needs to go it alone.

Another reason is that Russia needs to do something to make its vision for a Eurasian Economic Union far more attractive. A powerful army, cheap gas and promises from Moscow only go so far when it comes to enticing others to join a Russian-led economic bloc. This is perhaps one of the big lessons from the current Ukraine imbroglio – that Russia didn't make its vision for economic integration enticing enough. At the end of the day, would you rather trade with Kazakhstan and Belarus – or the European Union? When Ukraine wouldn't abandon its plans to join Europe, it only raised the stakes for Russia.

So think of what a Siberian project might do to enhance the appeal of a Eurasian Economic Union. Just as Sochi helped to showcase a "New Russia" to the world, complete with world-class venues, five-star accommodations and modern transportation links, the new "Sochi in Siberia" would also be based on a similar type of formula for success.

While this doesn't necessarily mean building massive, large-scale cities (as has often been proposed for Siberia), it would focus much more on developing infrastructure and transportation links that would connect Russia to the Far East and the Asia-Pacific. Russia has to be seen as an attractive trading and economic partner.

Finally, Russia can capitalize on Sochi infrastructure know-how immediately with proven partners like Russian Railways (formerly headed by close Putin ally Vladimir Yakunin) and Megafon. There's no denying that the vision for Sochi – the creation of two compact clusters of venues linked by high-speed train providing easy access to an international airport – has the potential to transform a region.

It took a lot of arm-twisting to get Russia's oligarchs to kick in money to finance all the infrastructure projects in Sochi, but the results were stunning. You can criticize Russia's foreign and domestic policies all you wanted, but you really can't criticize the planning and logistics that went into building a modern Sochi. (In fact, one of the signs that was prevalent at the Sochi Olympics was from Russian Railways, "We did everything, so that you would be first.")

The Sochi vision – and execution - was so compelling, in fact, that South Korea plans to copy it largely in whole when it hosts the PyeongChang Winter Olympics in 2018. In Sochi's Olympic Park, a pop-up "Korea House" detailed South Korea's plans for the next

Winter Olympics, and it was striking how much they appeared to emulate the Sochi model.

In PyeongChang, there will be a mountain cluster, a coastal cluster, and a new high-speed rail link. And, just as central Sochi acted as a cultural and economic anchor for development in Adler and Krasnaya Polyana, Korea is using Seoul (located 180 kilometers away) as an anchor for development throughout the region. In other words, the Sochi model works and it can be exported elsewhere.

The only question, really, is what a "Siberian Sochi" would look like. The Australian and Canadian models for developing vast, unpopulated areas received attention from Russian officials at the 2013 Krasnoyarsk Economic Forum.

But there's no reason why the new Sochi has to be located in Siberia. If you believe in the "Siberian Curse," maybe you'd prefer to construct Russia's next big economic showcase in the Arctic or in the Far East (i.e. Vladivostok).

The economic reality for Russia is that constructing these types of super-projects may provide the impetus for growth and development that a more organic Western model of modest growth, middle class development and small business creation hasn't thus far. It's hard to argue with 300 years of history.

From Dostoevsky to derivatives

Today, it's impossible to understand the nuances of modern Russia without having a top-flight knowledge of economics and finance. Not just classic microeconomics of the sort that you'd get in a university's Econ 101 class—but knowledge of currency markets, international debt markets, and modern commodity markets.

Today's Russia experts need this to understand all of the factors currently roiling modern Russia. Currency crises, sharp swings in the price of oil, free trade deals, debt downgrades, how equity markets react to political events—they're all topics that are helping to determine the arc of both Russian foreign and domestic policy.

During the heyday of the Cold War—and even in the two decades following the collapse of the Berlin Wall—Russian Studies programs in the United States typically required a mix of Russian language proficiency, knowledge of Russia's historical role in international affairs, a study of Russian culture (mostly 19th century literature, maybe some Solzhenitsyn or Pasternak thrown in for good measure), and enough knowledge of how the Soviet political system worked to make a few expert observations as a Kremlinologist.

That's a big problem for today's modern, interconnected world.

Notice what's missing—any type of broad-based understanding of global finance and macroeconomics. If you wanted to learn more about business in relation to Russia, it usually required taking MBA-level classes—and even these classes were usually found under the "emerging markets" rubric. There was no strong Russia focus. Even economic topics like "shock therapy" during the 1990s—which should have been studied from a macroeconomic perspective—tended to be approached from a sociological or historical perspective. (And look how "shock therapy" turned out.)

Consider the requirements for an undergraduate Russian Studies degree at Harvard, which has to be considered one of—if not the premier—Russian Studies program in the nation. As Harvard points out on the Davis Center website, "While the field may include the study of language, literature, and culture, the primary emphasis is on the social sciences, including history." While economics is one of the social sciences mentioned by Harvard, the others are anthropology, government and history. Harvard's two-year Master's Degree in Russia, Eastern Europe, and Central Asia (REECA) is no different. The program "offers advanced training in the history, politics, culture, society, and languages of this region." (But no economics or finance.)

If America's top Russian Studies programs won't guarantee their grads know as much about derivatives as Dostoevsky, you will get a strange bifurcation of "American expert opinion" about Russia.

On one hand, you will get the think tank experts and scholars rambling on about the Russian political system, liberally peppering their remarks about the grand sweep of Russian history or their in-depth knowledge of some intricate Cold War policy area, like strategic arms and nuclear disarmament. When it comes to economic solutions, they are still thinking in terms of the "shock therapy" solutions of the post-Soviet era, which they see in sociological or political terms rather than economic terms.

On the other hand, you get the traders and portfolio strategists who appear on CNBC and Bloomberg and in newspapers like the *Wall Street Journal*. These are the guys and girls who manage multi-million-dollar portfolios for a living, and for whom a drop in sovereign debt credit ratings has very real meaning—not just for average Russians, but also for institutional investors looking for juiced-up returns. These are the people who have an intuitive grasp of how oil prices fluctuate over time, and how the risk-reward premium differs across a variety of asset classes.

That sets up an odd contradiction in the Western capitalist system, as Lenin might have said.

At a time of potentially cataclysmic change in Russia (including intimations of regime change within the Kremlin), you have two very different sets of people trying to tell us what to do about Russia. You have the academics and scholars who pull out their Cold War frameworks and their knowledge of Russia's historical regimes from Peter the Great to Putin the Great. And then you have the Wall Street and London traders who have zero ideological baggage and actually might like Putin because he brings stability—the type of stability that is going to make them money in modern Russia.

So here's the solution: Make Econ 101 (and preferably, Finance 101) a minimum prerequisite for all Russian Studies grads. Encourage them to take classes in business and finance. The next generation of Russia experts should be able to discuss important topics like de-dollarization without blushing. They shouldn't flinch when they are asked to talk about oil derivatives such as futures, options and swaps. They should be able to make some truly informed opinions about deficits, borrowing costs, currency crises, free trade agreements and credit ratings.

The long-term benefits would be extraordinary—you'd be preparing the next generation of Russia experts not just for a career in academia and Think Tank Land (opportunities that really don't exist any more the way they did during the Cold War), but also to become consultants, traders, entrepreneurs and financiers. If the future of the U.S.-Russian relationship is in more business, more trade, and more economic relationships, this knowledge of macroeconomics and finance are vital not just for the future success of students, but also for the stability of the current world order.

U.S. sanctions against Russia: A tale of two cities

In many ways, New York and Washington couldn't be more different in how they view economic sanctions against Russia. While the Washington foreign policy elites are pushing to ramp up sanctions against Russia, arm Kiev and ostracize Russia on the world stage, it's a completely different scene in New York, where multinational managers, venture capitalists and institutional investors are looking for ways to roll back sanctions, find new avenues for business cooperation and integrate Russia into the global economy.

At Russia Forum New York 2015, hosted at the Princeton Club in midtown Manhattan by Russian Center New York, these differences between how the elites of Washington and New York view Russia came into stark contrast.

The event, which focused on the current Russian investment climate, consisted of a keynote by Russian Ambassador to the United States Sergey Kislyak and a set of three panels, each focusing on a different aspect of the U.S.-Russian business relationship: "Economic Cooperation," "Commerce and Innovation" and "Media and Business."

The Russia Forum New York followed the two-day World Russia Forum in Washington, which was organized by Edward Lozansky, president and founder of the American University in Moscow. This year's World Russia Forum marked the 35th annual meeting of the US-Russia Forum, dedicated to constructive dialogue in the U.S.-Russia relationship.

As Ambassador Kislyak noted in his opening remarks, Russia is still "open for business" and there's no need to fear a return of the Cold War even if the U.S. is attempting to isolate Russia both diplomatically and economically. The good news, Kislyak says, is that Russia is redoubling efforts at diversifying and modernizing its economy, including more emphasis on diversifying by geographic region.

As a result, the ruble has stabilized, the Russian economy is showing signs of positive growth in 2015 (even if it's "miserably low") and the feared credit crunch of February 2015 (when Russian companies were scheduled to pay back significant amounts of dollar-denominated debt) never materialized. In fact, Kislyak says, trade between the U.S. and Russia is still very much active, and actually increased by almost 5 percent in 2014, despite the U.S. economic sanctions against Russia.

And it's not just that economic sanctions against Russia are not having their desired effect. The U.S. policy of isolating Russia on the world stage may end up boomeranging and hitting the very people it was not supposed to impact – multinational companies that have invested in Russia for the long-haul, smaller companies, entrepreneurs, and young Russians who have embraced both globalization and innovation.

This was a complaint voiced continually at the forum, as speakers such as James Min of Deutsche Post DHL, Cyril Geacintov of DRG International and Dmitry Akhanov of Rusnano USA explained how sanctions have impacted their own businesses directly and why sanctions are hurting U.S. small business owners and young

Russian entrepreneurs far more than they are hurting Russia's largest state-backed corporations.

Even some Russian foreign policy insiders in Washington are starting to make this point. The most eloquent case for re-thinking sanctions was recently made by Samuel Charap, senior fellow for Russia and Eurasia at the International Institute for Strategic Studies, and Bernard Sucher in an op-ed for the *New York Times*: "Why Sanctions on Russia Will Backfire." Similar to the viewpoints expressed at the Russia Forum New York, Charap and Sucher argue that sanctions are impacting the wrong people and that they unfairly punish Russia for integrating into the global economy and embracing the American-led global financial system:

"While there is no question that sanctions have inflicted real costs on the leading state-owned and state-affiliated companies and harmed Mr. Putin's cronies, the collateral damage to independent, private enterprise in Russia is incomparably worse. Businesses without political protection will see atrophied sales, no access to finance and an indefinite postponement of investment. Those enterprises that put the greatest store on Russia's integration with the European Union and the United States are being hit hardest..."

So if sanctions against Russia don't make any sense, why pursue them?

The short answer is that sanctions are a form of low-hanging fruit for American politicians and diplomats, eager to show that that they are doing something – anything – to punish Russia for its annexation of Crimea and involvement in eastern Ukraine.

In many ways, though, the logic for this strategy can be traced back to a fundamental problem – there's simply not enough trade between Russia and the U.S. to make business incentives outweigh political incentives. Yes, trade between the U.S. and Russia may be growing, but total annual U.S.-Russian trade is estimated at only $40 billion by Russian Ambassador Sergey Kislyak. (By way of comparison, the Sochi Winter Olympics cost Russia $50 billion.) In terms of total annual U.S. trade, $40 billion is a drop in the bucket and a very easy way to punish Russia in a highly public manner.

The more complex answer as to why it's so hard to roll back sanctions now might be the systemic media bias within the American media industry. As John Varoli, a former journalist with the *New York Times* and *Bloomberg* pointed out in the panel on "Media and Business," this bias can be found across the media's ideological spectrum. The left-leaning media (*New York Times*, *Washington Post*) is pushing back against Russia's perceived conservatism and Eurasian values while the right-leaning media (*Wall Street Journal* and *The Economist*) is taking Russia to task for not having a full-fledged Western economic system.

Even on financial news networks such as CNBC or Bloomberg – media outlets that you might think would be sympathetic to the whole "Invest-in-an-emerging-market-like-Russia" thesis – you are going to find this bias. Look no further than hedge fund impresario Bill Browder, who has become the loudest and most passionate voice arguing for wrecking Russia's economy to punish Putin.

In the end, though, trying to wreck Russia and bring about regime change by using the economy as a foreign policy lever may backfire. As Marcos Troyjo, director of BRICLab, pointed out during his presentation at Russia Forum New York, we may be on the cusp of a fundamental change in the global economy driven by factors outside of the control of either Russia or the United States. Ukraine, now viewed as a geostrategic crisis, might one day be viewed more properly as a geo-economic crisis brought on by changes in how the world thinks about "deep globalization."

In 2015-2016, the world is likely to see a robust period of "re-globalization" featuring entirely new trade blocs (including, perhaps, the Eurasian Economic Union and the BRICS), the growth of an even more powerful China, and a shift from "comparative advantage" to "competitive advantage." As Troyjo noted, these factors could combine to create "new trade and investment geometries."

The hope in New York investment circles, of course, is that these changing geometries of capital flows will lead to changing geometries of political thinking. In other words, in a global financial system no longer created, run and controlled by America, there might be need to reassess where Russia stands in the global economy. And, as Derek Norberg, executive director of the Russian-American Pacific Partnership (RAPP) suggested in his presentation, that might be reason enough to stop giving Russia "the silent treatment" when it comes to possible economic cooperation.

But it will take time for any of this political thinking to take hold. The Washington foreign policy elites are still all dialed into the triumphalism of the Cold War. None of the speakers at the Russia Forum New York seemed overly optimistic that a fundamental mindset change could happen during the current Obama administration – and maybe not even if Republicans win the presidency in 2016.

What it might take is a new, non-interventionist candidate such as Rand Paul and an American electorate tired of endless wars in Afghanistan, Iraq and Syria for any attempt to rollback policies that punish Russia's business leaders rather than Russia's government elite.

At the end of the day, it's up to America's business leaders to change the narrative about Russia. Natalie Sabelnik, chair of the Coordinating Council of Russian Compatriots in the U.S., suggested at the Russia Forum New York that "this is the window of opportunity" for Russian and American business leaders. In short, we've had one year to see that sanctions have not been successful.

This potential mindset change, whether hopeful or real, is highly evocative of Charles Dickens and his famous opening lines of "The Tale of Two Cities." How will leaders in New York and Washington choose to view Russia?

When it comes to the U.S.-Russian relationship, are we currently experiencing "the worst of times" (as the Washington elite would suggest) or is it the "best of times" (as Russia's investors, entrepreneurs and small business owners would suggest)? Is it the "age of foolishness" or the "age of wisdom"? And, most importantly, will the "winter of despair" be followed by a "spring of hope"?

A Cure For Russophobia

"Russia cannot be understood with the mind alone, No ordinary yardstick can span her greatness: She stands alone, unique. In Russia, one can only believe."

- Fyodor Tyutchev (1803-1873)

The Sochi Olympics promised an Opening Ceremony for the New Russia

The spectacular Opening Ceremony for the Sochi 2014 Winter Olympics was supposed to mark the start of a new, more confident role for Russia on the global stage. In many ways, the Sochi Olympics were the ultimate attempt to boost the country's soft power in the world and cure the West of its Russophobia.

The Sochi Winter Olympics were always about showcasing a new, dynamic Russia to the world. Starting with the dramatic Opening Ceremony – which showcased Russia's prowess not only in athletics but also in culture, science, the arts and engineering – the Sochi 2014 Winter Olympics were all about challenging the legacy assumptions about Russia that are holdovers from the Cold War and post-Cold War period.

It's almost as if the old symbols of Russia were updated with vibrant colors and a massive, thumping techno beat. There was color everywhere you looked at the Opening Ceremony, starting with the initial sequence celebrating the Cyrillic alphabet and ending with the lighting of the Olympic Flame and the fireworks above Fisht stadium. Classic Russian folk song were often re-interpreted with a contemporary, techno beat, and songs like t.A.T.u.'s "Not gonna get us," were interwoven into the arrival of the Russian Olympic team at the stadium.

And that color and sound remained in place throughout the Sochi 2014 Winter Olympics. Most notably, there were 25,000 volunteers dressed in bright festive uniforms celebrating the colorful designs of all the regions of Russia. These volunteers were everywhere you looked – on the streets, at the venues, at the rail stations, and at the airport. The Sochi 2014 branding – the color patchwork design – was also installed at every competition venue, in shades of vibrant purples, greens, yellows and blues.

At night, the competition venues in the Olympic Park were transformed by colorful lighting displays, including a 3D light show on the walls of the Iceberg Skating Palace, where Russia's 15-year-old Yulia Lipnitskaya became the world's newest figure skating sensation. In the mountains, dramatic pastel lighting illuminated the new ski resort areas of Krasnaya Polyana. People who were expecting tried-and-true Russian folk symbols from the 19th century may have been surprised at just how modernistic and bright everything appeared to be.

At the same time, there was a new can-do dynamism in Sochi. Russia's old inferiority complex of the post-Cold War era, when it was forced to import Western expertise – as well as Western words – to make up for lost time during the final years of the Soviet Union, seems to be replaced with a bit of swagger.

Throughout the Opening Ceremony, signs and symbols of Russia's achievements were everywhere – from the arts to the sciences to the exploration of the cosmos. And that was carried through to the Olympic competitions. At sporting events during the two weeks of competition, fans launched into spirited chants of "Rossiya" every time a Russian champion took to the ice.

While the Opening Ceremony was a celebration of how the New Russia sees itself in the world, it doesn't mean that Russia has turned its back on the Soviet era. This, in many ways, was one of the most surprising aspects of the Opening Ceremony – how much

Russia celebrated its massive achievements of the Soviet Era. And it did it in a way that was both inspiring and fun – such as the arrival of Moscow's dancing "stilyagi" ("hipsters") and Soviet-era baby carriages along with powerful symbols of Soviet-era transformation.

There's a lot of powerful nostalgia from that era when the Soviet Union was a global superpower, and Vladimir Putin's Russia is no longer afraid to tap into that powerful reservoir of national pride. This is a marked change from the twenty-year period from 1992-2012, when it seemed like Russia could do nothing right, and was often forced into the role of a supplicant of the West, dependent on foreign aid, foreign expertise and foreign guidance.

There is even a famous saying from that era, usually attributed to Viktor Chernomyrdin, that encapsulates the fatalism of that time: "Things started off good, but ended up the way they always do." That's no longer true – people fully expected Russia to medal in every event, and fans were wowed by the scope and scale of the venues in the new Olympic Park.

Once the Winter Olympics came to a close, Russia was hoping that it would have new friends in the world, especially in places like Korea and China, where huge audiences were tuning in to watch their national champions compete in Sochi. Korean journalists and Olympic officials showed up in force in Sochi as they prepare for the arrival of the Winter Olympics in 2018. That goodwill with Asian nations could be key for Russia, as it seeks a way to pivot to Asia and engage new trading partners. Getting deals done in Asia doesn't come with the same baggage that getting deals done in Europe does these days.

Russia also hoped that many of the legacy assumptions of the Cold War era may finally be overturned. In Sochi, people were smiling, celebrating and enjoying the global spotlight as the whole world tunes in to see what Russia has accomplished. Visitors, it was thought, would return to their home countries, sharing their stories of Russia was different from how they originally imagined.

What we saw, in reality, was a more muscular Russian foreign policy presence on the global stage. Pulling off the Olympics in style meant that Russia had a newfound confidence in the diplomatic realm and an increasing number of opportunities to transform its ambitions into reality.

The strange rise and fall of Russian soft power

Nobody could have predicted the events that followed within weeks of the conclusion of the Sochi 2014 Winter Olympics – the appearance of "little green men" in Crimea and the annexation of part of Ukraine, followed shortly thereafter by the arrival of masked separatists in eastern Ukraine. All of a sudden, any talk of Russian soft power seemed almost anachronistic.

For Russia, soft power is turning out to be another of those Western liberal-democratic ideals that was imported to the nation during the 1990s and that never turned out the way it was supposed to. "Soft power" (coined in 1990 by Harvard professor Joseph Nye) ranks right up there with "Shock Therapy" (coined by another Harvard professor, Jeffrey Sachs, during the Gorbachev-Yeltsin years) as an idea that sounded good at the time, but turned out to be completely wrong for Russia.

In the latest Soft Power 30 Index, released by the Portland communications agency in mid-2015, Russia didn't even make the cut of the Top 30 nations in the world. Instead of embracing the latest feel-good theories of Ivy League academics, Russia has embraced the cold, hard logic of international relations realists. Now that we've woken up to the fact that the "End of History" (another brilliant theory, by the way, that turned out to be false) is no longer nigh, we can stop figuring out how Russia can transform itself to look like a carbon copy of America.

It's no longer the 1990s, with apologies to Joseph Nye, who also wrote the introduction to the latest Soft Power Rankings. Didn't 9/11 wake us up to that fact almost 15 years ago? In a dangerous world of the Islamic State of Iraq and the Greater Syria (ISIS) and Al-Qaeda, gas pipelines and guns – classic "hard power" – go a lot further than "soft power" does these days. Just consider how much return of investment (ROI) Russia got on its Sochi 2014 soft power project. The West didn't even want to show up, no matter that Russia spent close to $50 billion throwing the blowout party of the year.

Let's be realists here for a second. Offering to build a massive gas pipeline through your country exerts an extraordinary amount of influence these days in national political circles. Just ask China, India, Turkey, Greece, Ukraine or just about any nation in Europe these days. In the same way, other levers of economic influence – such as trade partnerships and economic development deals – go a lot further than ever before. No wonder Russia is scrambling to beef up the Eurasian Economic Union and China is working to build out its Silk Road project.

And, if all else fails, exporting guns, armor and tanks works fine, too. Who needs the Winter Olympics and biathlon events held high up in the snowy peaks of Sochi when you can host the World Tank Biathlon in Moscow and attract non-NATO nations to check out your military hardware instead? Check out all the places in the world where Russian "hard power" is winning friends and gaining influence. Consider Iran, for example. Russian political values matter a lot less than the ability to build nuclear power plants and arm the nation with the latest missiles.

That's why it's hard to believe the latest Soft Power 30 Index reflects the current international trends. It suffers the fate of all the other soft power rankings that have ever been released – it sounds more like a suggested tourism agenda for a grand European tour than a reflection of today's geostrategic realities. Consider some of the names that cracked the Top 20... Spain? Ireland? Belgium? Italy?

Get this, Greece somehow managed to crack the list of Top 25 soft power nations in the world. Yes, the beaches of Santorini are nice this time of year – but it's hard to believe that Greece has any kind of soft power influence these days when the banks don't even open some days and the country is on the edge of an epic financial meltdown.

Which brings us to the core problem with this soft power index. Just consider how Euro-centric and Western-centric the whole index is. In the Top 20, there are only two non-Western nations: Japan and South Korea. Consider all the nations that should have been part of the conversation, but weren't. China ranks #30 in the world in terms of soft power, really?

These soft power rankings – far from showing how far Russia has fallen in its soft power ambitions - is further proof of how the Western world is still unable to comprehend the rise of China, the BRICS and the non-Western world. It's no wonder they still view Russian strategic moves through a Cold War prism – they haven't yet grasped that China has more influence and power in the world today than, say, Denmark (#11). For that matter, how did Poland (#24) and the Czech Republic (#27) crack the Top 30? If we're defining soft power as the ability to influence and win over people, what is Poland or the Czech Republic doing right that Russia isn't?

As a measure of soft power in the West, the ranking certainly has its merits. It does neatly define the core components of soft power and makes the case that digital assets matter today more than ever (perhaps not so surprising, given that Facebook was one of the co-creators of the ranking).

However, this Soft Power 30 rankings doesn't take into account Russia's new pivot away from the West, and the way this changes Russian thinking about global influence. Russia seems to have given up on the West, booting out American NGOs and then gloating about it. Yes, agreed, it's heartbreaking to watch happen.

But what about China? Turkey? The BRICS? Russia doesn't have time to build up the type of reputation and influence in these nations that are representative of classic soft power – it needs to act now. It needs to do deals, whether economic or military. The student exchanges and scientific exchanges will come later.

At the end of the day, "soft power" is really a brilliant innovation to explain and perpetuate America's dominant role in the world. "Soft power" makes a global hegemon sound like a gentle giant. Just as Britain was forced to come up with a justification for its global empire before it faded from the world stage more than a century ago, America is looking for a way to justify its role as a global empire now – and a theory by a famous Harvard professor is as good as any. More than 100 years ago, the British imperialists would have been telling the good people of India and Africa about "British soft power" and why they should remain under British colonial control. Britain, by the way, ranked #1 in the soft power index, so maybe they are still doing something right around the world.

With time, of course, it's possible to see the blurry outlines of the next push for Russian soft power. First, Russia has got to resolve the Ukraine crisis. Then, it has to figure out if the BRICS are really going to change the world. And it has to figure out what to do about Central Asia, the Middle East and the pivot to Asia. The exact form that Russian soft power will take in the future is not certain – it may borrow from the "Russian World" concept much in vogue these days, or from "Russian Orthodoxy" or from "Eurasianism" – but one thing is certain: it will always play second fiddle to the traditional instruments of Russian hard power: guns and pipelines.

Remember what former U.S. President Teddy Roosevelt once said about foreign policy? "Speak softly, and carry a big stick." For nearly a decade, Russia tried to speak softly, but nobody listened. Now it's carrying a big stick.

Engage the Russian bear, don't isolate it

At the 34th annual meeting of the World Russia Forum in Washington in 2014, participants discussed a constructive agenda for U.S.-Russian relations that included ideas for expanding links in fields ranging from economics and business to art, culture and technology. If there's one theme that emerged the event, it's that Russia and the United States are more interconnected than you might think.

In short, instead of enraging the Russian bear, the U.S. should be seeking ways of engaging it.

While trade and economic relations between the two nations are still at a relatively undeveloped level and under constant threat from sanctions, it's clear that there are a growing number of areas where the two nations might cooperate – everything from joining forces in the war against terrorism to developing the Arctic together, creating new educational exchanges, or partnering on new technological innovation.

And the more the two countries combine and collaborate, the less the chances of an event like Ukraine spiraling into an international crisis and launching daily discussions of a new Cold War.

The event, organized by Edward Lozansky, president of the American University in Moscow, the Eurasia Center, and the Russian Center NY – an event that the *Washington Times* called a "major Washington conference on bilateral relations" – featured no less than three ambassadors (current Russian Ambassador Sergey Kislyak and former Russian Ambassador Vladimir Lukin, former Ambassador Jack Matlock from the U.S.), the appearance of major Russia scholars (Stephen Cohen, Robert Legvold), and even an old school "tele-most" between the United States and Russia organized by Interfax in Moscow.

The "tele-most" event, moderated by Edward Lozansky in Washington, led to a few lighthearted comments about the impact of Western sanctions since one of the speakers – Sergey Mironov of the Russian Duma – happens to be one of the unfortunate Russian individuals on the U.S. sanctions list.

In the keynote that led off the event, Ambassador Kislyak outlined the ways that Russia and the U.S. need to collaborate. He also discounted any notion that the U.S. and Russia were locked in any form of a "new Cold War," stating that there was "not a single ideological issue" that separates the two sides. And former U.S. Ambassador to Russia Jack Matlock – who experienced a real Cold War first-hand – called it a "travesty" that we were even trying to call this period a "Cold War." What is needed, he said, was more types of cultural exchanges between the two countries.

It's no wonder a big part of the first day of the event was attempting to define what type of period we are in right now, with some of the options being "Cold War II," an "inter-Cold War period," and a "new Cold War." Even the Russian experts disagreed amongst themselves. Cohen argued that we're not in a Cold War, while Legvold pointed to his latest piece ("Managing a New Cold War") in *Foreign Affairs*, in which he describes a new Cold War without any ideological basis.

What's clear at many levels is that many in the United States do not understand either the intensity of Russian involvement in

Ukraine, or the way that Russia views its stake in the region. Outside of the Beltway, said Ambassador Matlock, people in America don't even know that we're in a Cold War.

Time and time again, speakers mentioned the need to recalibrate expectations. The only problem is, the Obama Administration shows little or no willingness to engage in dialogue, while mainstream media continues to marginalize any Western experts who attempt to explain the Kremlin's position. And, to top it all off, the U.S. still doesn't have an Ambassador to Russia yet. That makes it tough to work things out in private.

A number of theories were advanced as to the big disconnect between American foreign policy and Russian foreign policy, with the most likely being that too many top Russia scholars have been marginalized by the mainstream media.

Cohen, hitting back at critics who have variously labeled him a "dupe" and a "Putin apologist," offered up an assessment of the current landscape from a number of different perspectives. He basically called the World Russia Forum a call-to-arms for Russia policy "heretics" who were tired of being excluded from airing their opinions in the mainstream media.

The emerging consensus – offered up both by Russian and American participants – was that it was better off including Russia going forward rather than attempting to isolate it. Ambassador Kislyak, quoted in the *Wall Street Journal*, made it clear that sanctions were not the way forward.

Former Russian PM Sergey Stepashin, in the tele-most, even suggested that sanctions were "medieval" in nature, a relic of past history. Mironov, himself stuck on the U.S. sanctions list, argued that no sanctions would work, ever, against Russia.

One of the more entertaining discussions of sanctions came from Leonid Gozman, the president of the Union of Right Forces (SPS) opposition movement in Russia.

Calling himself one of the 1 percent of people who doesn't agree with Russia's actions in Crimea, Gozman outlined why the U.S. strategy of surgical sanctions were almost certain to hurt Vladimir Putin's inner circle but could not hurt Putin himself.

So if sanctions are not the way forward, then what? The key will be forming more types of collaborations and linkages between the U.S. and Russia, in spheres ranging from education and culture to science and technology.

The more these types of collaborations are formed, the more there will be room to work around difficult down times in relationship. Panelists at the event included those building educational linkages between Russian universities and top American universities, as well as Rita Guenther, a program officer from the National Academy of Sciences, who described efforts to keep the dialogue open between U.S. and Russian scientists.

For better or worse, Russia and U.S. will be at loggerheads in other regions of world – Asia, Central Asia and Europe – so the two sides had better get used to working together. In fact, in one of the more audacious concepts floated at event (first humorously, then rather seriously), was the notion of a tunnel linking Chukotka in Russia and Alaska. To make the concept all the more real, Alaska Lt. Governor Mead Treadwell outlined five key areas where his state was looking to partner with Russia, including the Arctic.

One of the more entertaining talks was given by Minnesota Secretary of State Mark Ritchie, who talked about ways that he had to get around the order from Washington that business dealings with the Russians were to be ignored.

In fact, he went ahead with plans to host an innovation conference with Russian startups and venture capital investors that ended up attracting 300 people. He named a number of Minnesota-based companies – like Cargill and 3M – that are interested in partnering with Russian business, and even went so far as to give a shout-out to all the ways that his state is culturally (and linguistically) prepared to reach out to colleagues in Russia.

He wasn't the only one pitching the idea for business collaboration. From the Russian side, one comment was that "money doesn't smell." In other words, who cares what's happening in the realm of politics, as long as there is money to be made?

Panelists talked up the need for infrastructure development in Russia and the innovation potential of Russian start-ups and scientific establishments.

And, in fact, one big theme that emerged – especially in the final session of the program – was that Western oil & gas giants had too much money at stake to let their Russian partners walk away. Ralph Winnie, Jr. of the Eurasia Center described the potential to create a Russian "shale gas revolution" that would dwarf the size of the American shale gas revolution, while others talked up the prospects for Arctic oil and gas exploration.

What will be interesting is how these opportunities for collaboration – both business and political – are developed over next few months. There was already chatter about restoring the East-West Accord meetings from the old Cold War days, something that actually became a reality in 2015.

The best hope is that this talk gets pushed to a wider audience, beyond just the marginalized Russia experts in the U.S. – perhaps even to Obama's inner circle, who will find ways to meet one-on-one with their Russian colleagues before events in eastern Ukraine spiral out of control.

Burger diplomacy: From Big Mac to Shake Shack

Despite the seemingly vast ideological gap that now exists between Moscow and Washington and all the talk of a new Cold War, there is still hope that the members of the younger generation in both Russia and the United States can change how we think about geopolitics and foreign policy. The world is flat now, and that means that the future members of the political elites in both Moscow and Washington look, act, and think much more alike than perhaps at any time in history.

During the Cold War, the opening of the first McDonald's in the center of Moscow in 1990 just months before the collapse of the Soviet Union became a metaphor for America's cultural triumph over tired Soviet dogmatism. Over the next 20 years, McDonald's would open more than 200 locations across Russia, becoming the new face of American capitalism to millions of Russians who were coming into contact with the West for the first time. If then-Soviet President Nikita Khrushchev and his U.S. counterpart Nixon had their version of "kitchen diplomacy," then Reagan and Gorbachev had what can only be referred to as "burger diplomacy."

That was then, this is now.

The "burger diplomacy" of the new generation will most likely involve something like Shake Shack – the phenomenally popular upscale burger joint founded by Danny Meyer in New York City that has become something of a cultural phenomenon. What started with one location in Madison Square Park in New York has now expanded both nationally and internationally. There are Shake Shack locations in Washington - including one close to the

Russian Embassy - and another that opened in Moscow on the city's flashy Novy Arbat. Theoretically, an international jetsetter could now travel from New York to London to Abu Dhabi to Moscow and then back to Washington, consuming Shack Burgers each step of the way.

While talking about "burger diplomacy" might seem a bit out of place amongst all the high-level diplomatic meetings that take place in Moscow, Washington, Vienna, Paris and Geneva, "burger diplomacy" actually holds a greater lesson – and that is that the new young elites that are emerging in New York and Moscow and Washington actually have more in common than we might imagine. They increasingly have the same educational backgrounds, the same travel experiences and the same leisure preferences.

In January 2011, Chrystia Freeland of *The Atlantic* wrote an article about "the rise of the new global elite" – a group of high-powered jetsetters that travel effortlessly between the major capitals of the world, vacationing in Abu Dhabi, buying espresso in Rome and eating out in New York.

As wealth differentials continue to grow in societies around the world, the important takeaway is that the average member of the Russian elite and the average member of the Western elite perhaps now have more in common with each other than they do with their fellow citizens.

A member of the global elite in New York likely understands the concerns of a fellow member of the global elite in Moscow better than the concerns of a farmer in Iowa. They are educated at the same schools, work for the same global companies, go on holiday in the same locations, and, yes, they eat the same burgers.

The only question remaining is, "What do we call this new global elite"? As early as 2008, David Rothkopf referred to the global "super class," which he defines as the Top 6000 wealthiest and most powerful people in the world.

If you buy into the "Big Mac to Shake Shack" concept, it's likely that the number is much higher than this. After all, it's not like the Shake Shack is meant to be an elite institution – on the website for the Moscow location, they even refer to themselves as "the people's patty." Take that Politburo!

Until the imposition of economic sanctions (followed by Russian counter-sanctions), McDonald's had not lost a step in Russia. Even more than 20 years later, the McDonald's on Moscow's Pushkin Square – in the very heart of Moscow, within a five-minute walk of Red Square and the Kremlin – remained the chain's busiest location in the world – serving over 40,000 people every day.

Yet, McDonald's no longer has the same hold on the mindset of the average Russian. McDonald's is no longer a cultural signifier the way it used to be. McDonald's is now more of an economic signifier – a realization that, for the West, Russia is now one of the world's most attractive economic markets and the source of a brand new consumer base.

The opening of the Shake Shack in Moscow is just the latest step in the flattening of the world for the people at the top of the economic pyramid. We could just as easily be talking about Starbucks and Apple instead of Shake Shack – just as we could have been talking about Pepsi and Levi's instead of McDonald's a generation ago.

The transition from Big Mac to Shake Shack has important implications for the way we think not only about relations between the U.S. and Russia, but also geopolitics in general. A whole new generation of "hardworking, highly educated, jet-setting meritocrats who feel they are the deserving winners of a tough, worldwide economic competition" are changing the way we think about the world.

If the former paradigm for understanding the world was developed vs. underdeveloped country, or West vs. East, or Democracy vs. Authoritarianism or Capitalism vs. Communism, something very new is emerging in capitals around the world, linking New York and Washington with London and Paris, but also Moscow, Mumbai, Rio, and Shanghai. It might just be possible that today's young overachievers in New York and Moscow end up being global partners rather than global rivals.

Why we need a Great American Novel about Russia

How the rise of a new global elite plays out in foreign affairs – and specifically, in U.S.-Russian relations – is yet to be seen. However, it is likely that we will begin to see the first signs of changing perceptions about Russia in fields that thrive on person-to-person exchanges, such as science, culture and the arts. Imagine American films and books filled with positive stereotypes about Russia, rather than negative stereotypes. Or, best of all, imagine a Great American Novel that explains the complexities of modern Russia.

One writer who comes to mind is Jonathan Franzen, who's generally considered one of America's greatest living novelists. His new novel "Purity" released in September 2015 is almost certain to be another bestseller, following in the footsteps of "The Corrections" and "Freedom."

The important thing you need to know is that Franzen really, really wants to visit Russia. We know this because Franzen has told us this. In the September 2015 issue of *Conde Nast Traveler* (where his essay on bird-watching in East Africa also appears), he says that, of all the places in the world, the one place that he's "embarrassed" (his word, not mine) he's never been is Russia.

Why Russia? It turns out that three of Franzen's Top 10 favorite novels of all time are Russian. There's "Brothers Karamazov" (#1), "War and Peace" (#2) and "Lolita" (#8). It's easy to see why— Franzen's sprawling, big idea novels spanning several different generations are probably as close as an American writer can come to replicating the style of a sprawling, big idea Russian novel spanning several different generations.

In his novel "Freedom," Franzen even uses Russian literary allusions to "War and Peace" to describe the thoughts and feelings of his characters. That's because the characters in "War and Peace," Franzen says, "struggle with love and with finding the right way to live" —two themes that he covers in his own novels.

He's also a big fan of Russian literary theory. In the way that he tackles bigger social issues, Franzen is like the great Russian authors who try to change society. Franzen is the type of "important writer" who pens cultural essays for *Harper's* or *The New Yorker* on topics ranging from America's dysfunctional capitalist system to the role of the writer in modern society. He's at home talking about ideas, and how these ideas transform across cultures and between generations.

As a result, Franzen's take on modern Russia would be so much more relevant than that provided by today's mainstream media or Washington's think tanks, because it would go so deep into the dysfunctional nature of modern Russia. Franzen could offer more than just a rhetorical attack on modern Russia—it would be a nuanced take on Russian culture, Russian ideas and the evolving nature of power and capitalism in modern Russia.

In a much-discussed 1996 *Harper's* essay ("Perchance to Dream"), Franzen referred to "the burden of newsbringing." What he meant was that, in traditional literature, it was the duty of the novelist to instruct readers about what was wrong with their world, not just to entertain them. That duty, though, has become harder and harder, due to the onslaught of the Internet and digital media, says

Franzen. But it's clear that's where Franzen's heart is—to tell these types of stories.

Interestingly, using this definition of "newsbringing," you could define a number of modern Russian literary giants as "newsbringers." The best example might be Alexander Solzhenitsyn, who instructed readers of the horrors of the Russian gulag system within the format of the novel. In this group of Russian "newsbringers," you could add any of the Soviet-era writers who used the novel to expose the falsities of the Soviet Union, such as Trifonov ("House on the Embankment") or Platonov ("The Foundation Pit").

So what might an epic Franzen novel about Russia look like? Based on clues in his new novel "Purity," there are three possible directions a novel about Russia might take.

The novel might be a modern version of Dostoevsky's "Crime and Punishment." We already know that Franzen is a big fan of Dostoevsky's "Brothers Karamazov" and that Dostoevsky is the type of writer who would surely resonate with Franzen. (Back in the day, wearing a wearing a black turtleneck, reading Dostoevsky and drinking an espresso was enough to be called an "intellectual" at just about any American liberal arts university.)

And, in Franzen's new book "Purity," there's a scene that reminds the *Wall Street Journal*'s Sam Sacks of Dostoevsky's classic "Crime and Punishment":

"It's in dramatizing the murder that he plunges into deeper psychological waters than he has previously explored. This long, gripping scene is an almost second-by-second enactment of the preparation, act and aftermath of the killing. The atmosphere of terror and bewilderment calls to mind Dostoevsky's "Crime and Punishment."

As a result, a Franzen take on "Crime and Punishment" might analyze all the societal factors at work within Putin's Russia, just as Dostoevsky sought out answers about imperial Russia.

Another option might be a sprawling novel featuring Edward Snowden, Russia's Internet censors, and Moscow's democracy activists. Throughout "Purity," one plot line features a group of young anarchists and Internet activists. This second option, then, might focus on the story of a Russian opposition member in Moscow, bitter and powerless against the Leviathan state. After all, the heroine of "Purity" is a 20-something anarchist ("Pip" Tyler) looking for a lifeline while confronting limited future prospects.

In "Purity," there's also mention of a Julian Assange-type figure running a WikiLeaks-like organization called the Sunlight Project. What better way to spin a gripping tale of Russia's embittered democracy activists, than to recount how they do battle with Russia's Internet censor, Roskomnadzor? There would be accounts of Reddit, Wikipedia and Vkontakte (Russia's Facebook) as they attempt to outwit the Russian state.

Finally, Franzen might opt for an epic tale of power in Putin's Russia spanning several generations. Imagine "The Corrections" transplanted to Moscow. Or "Freedom" as told through the eyes of disillusioned members of the Russian middle class in cities such as St. Petersburg, Moscow and Sochi. There would be room for vast plot twists and character development over successive generations—from imperial Russia to Soviet Russia to Putinist

Russia. Given Franzen's love of birds, he could even spin in an apocryphal account of Putin's flight with the Siberian cranes.

This last option — an epic tale of power in Putin's Russia spanning several generations — might be the most instructive for today's current crop of Russia-watchers. It might help to introduce some nuances into a discussion of modern Russia — an acute sense of the loss of empire that began in the late 1980s, the disillusionment that followed the initial euphoria of Western capitalism in the 1990s, and the rise of nationalist, great power ambitions within Russia in the 2000s.

Let's hope that Franzen some day finds a way to make it to Russia and write a book with weighty Russian concepts such as "freedom" (свобода) or "purity" (чистота) at its core. The next great American novel might just end up being the next great Russian novel, that is, if Franzen's editor doesn't talk him out of it.

From Russia, with T-shirt

Forget about hosting another $50 billion Olympics – it might just be the case that the best Russian soft power is a $5 soft cotton t-shirt. Consider that, on his recent diplomatic trip to Russia in May 2015, John Kerry received a Victory Day t-shirt (and a basket of Sochi tomatoes) from his Russian counterpart Sergey Lavrov. That's a small step forward in t-shirt diplomacy, but it does hint that Cold War rivals Russia and the United States may actually have more in common than is often supposed.

What's needed, however, is an entirely new aesthetic for Russian t-shirts. Those "Pobeda" t-shirts commemorating the 70th anniversary of Victory Day that Lavrov offered up are ghastly— it's hard to imagine anyone—even patriotic Russians - walking around with those t-shirts.

Garish as they are, "Victory Day" t-shirts are a step above the t-shirts adorned with images of Vladimir Putin that are apparently popular in Russia these days.

The problem is that, when it comes to Russian t-shirt design, there are basically two alternatives—the kitschy Soviet t-shirt (think "McLenin's") or the over-the-top tackiness that results when you mash up Western pop culture with Russian political culture. Walk down the Arbat in central Moscow (or visit any tourist attraction in Russia), and there are slim pickings indeed for a Western tourist wanting to take home a little slice of authentic Russian culture.

So here's one idea: create an entirely new Russian t-shirt aesthetic that changes the perceptions of Russia without being overtly political. Something that you might actually want to wear around downtown Manhattan without being called out as some kind of Putin apologist.

Something that involves a warm, cuddly Russian bear, combined with a Western pop culture meme – something along the lines of "Make Music, Not War" - might just work.

The reason is that this t-shirt design would combine instantly recognizable Russian iconography — say, a bear and balalaika — without overtly mentioning Russia. The design would soften the Russian grizzly bear, turning it into a cuddly cub strumming away on a balalaika in the Ukrainian woods. And it would use the well-known message of "Make Music Not War," making it socially acceptable to wear the shirt around in public to protest American military intervention in Ukraine. Hey, even if you're not a big Russophile, nobody likes war, right?

It's easy to see how this design aesthetic could be adopted over and over again, using similar types of instantly recognizable Russian iconography. It's possible to imagine Russia-themed t-shirts with Bolshoi ballet dancers, Sputnik satellites, Russian samovars, or snowy wintry scenes with troikas.

You see this type of t-shirt all the time in the U.S. from big soft power nations. The classic American retailer Gap does this for the British and the French. For example, you'll see a graphic of an Eiffel Tower and a simple phrase like "Je t'aime" or "Bonjour." You might not like the skinny, baguette-eating French, but it's hard to argue with a phrase that simply says "I Love You" or "Hello."

Why can't Russia do this same type of thing as part of a new soft power campaign? Imagine onion domes and a friendly Russian message ("I love you") that's been scrubbed of any ideological meaning. From Russia with Love. And t-shirt, too.

Curing the mainstream media of its Russophobia

As the U.S. and Russia inch ever closer to full-fledged military confrontation over Ukraine, there are the first signs of true dialogue on U.S.-Russian relations. And it's not just U.S. Secretary of State John Kerry popping in to say "hi" in Sochi. After more than a year of being marginalized by the mainstream media – and some would say, even ostracized by their peers – respected foreign policy analysts presenting more nuanced views on Russia are finally appearing both online and in print.

One recent example is James Carden's controversial piece for *The Nation* during summer 2015. In it, he hits back hard at the anti-Russian bias in the Western media, something that he says has the potential to morph into a neo-McCarthyism of the type that we last witnessed during the Cold War era.

One article, of course, does not a trend make. However, consider some of the other pieces that have recently appeared either online or in print. You have Stephen F. Cohen warning about anti-Russian bias in an April 2015 interview with Salon. On the May/June 2015 cover of *The American Interest*, you have Stephen Sestanovich suggesting that the West might have provoked Russia.

And, most recently, you have Mark Ames for Pando Daily mounting a colossal takedown of the pro-war, pro-regime change neoconservative movement in America, which now seems to be behind much of the political lobbying urging America on to war in Europe.

The big question, of course, is whether this is just the flare-up of marginalized voices on the sidelines of American foreign policy. Or is this part of a bigger trend?

Critics, of course, could easily point out that the only reason the Carden piece in *The Nation* saw the light of day is because of the relationship between *The Nation* and Stephen F. Cohen, still one of the nation's most prominent Russia scholars and also, by the way, the husband of *The Nation* editor and publisher Katrina vanden Heuvel.

But if you take a look at the unexpected arrival of new voices on the media scene, it's clear that something unique is happening. Alternative viewpoints, once on the extreme, now have a much higher chance of getting into the mainstream. Ideas, opinions and logic are starting to supplant pure "propaganda," either pro-Russian or anti-Russian. And, most importantly, more nuanced views that take into account both Russian and American viewpoints are now being added to the mix.

What's making all this possible, most likely, is the severity of the current Ukraine crisis – we are so close to war that cooler heads may actually be prevailing. The steady drumbeat of military anniversaries – the 100th anniversary of the start of World War I, the 70th anniversary of the end of World War II, the 70th anniversary of the United Nations - has woken some from a slumber.

As a result, anti-war voices are being added to the mix, adding new heft and weight. Take former Soviet leader Mikhail Gorbachev, for example, who has weighed in time and time again on the perils of underestimating Putin and Russia.

To understand why the Carden piece in *The Nation* was so controversial, it's helpful to think about the media purely in terms of how they influence the political debate within America. In order for any new idea or concept to make it into everyday debate, it usually travels a path from the non-mainstream media to the mainstream media. At each step of this journey, the idea is further refined or broken down by experts and commentators and bloggers, such that it can be talked about easily at an evening cocktail party with a few pithy sound bites.

Thus, you have two key pieces in understanding the strange appearance of real dialogue about U.S.-Russian relations.

First, you have the non-mainstream media, which is helpful in its own way as a feeder of ideas and talent into splinter political groups and movements. You can think of the non-mainstream media in terms of blogs, social media, alternative news sites and online communities – all of which eventually filter into TV, newspapers and magazines.

And then you have the mainstream media, which you can think about in terms of the *New York Times* and *Washington Post* and *Wall Street Journal*. This mainstream media also includes the big "ideas" magazines that you see on the bookshelf of a typical Barnes & Noble bookstore. As a basic rule of thumb: If you don't see it on a magazine shelf at Barnes & Noble, it isn't mainstream.

Once you think about the media in this way – as a continuum of influence (or, if you prefer, a "stream" of influence) - it's easy to erect a heavily fortified Maginot Line down the middle, separating mainstream from non-mainstream. Nothing gets into the mainstream without a fight.

On one side of the continuum, you have RT (formerly Russia Today) and a bunch of pro-Russia conspiracy websites. Then, as you head further along the continuum, you start to see a growing number of pro-Russia blogs and pro-Russia communities. In this grouping, you can add media sites such as Russia Insider, which just ran a highly successful crowdfunding project on Kickstarter to challenge mainstream media bias on Russia.

Then, as you pass through the Maginot Line dividing mainstream from non-mainstream, you have "ideas" magazines like *The Nation* and *The New Yorker* and *The Atlantic*, most of them monthly or quarterly, all with big online audiences. Then, as you head even further along the continuum, you run into daily newspapers and the big online destinations for news. The gold standard, though, will always be the *New York Times* or *Washington Post*.

What's happened, apparently, is that Stephen F. Cohen and like-minded thinkers are starting to have their ideas picked up by blogs and social media, and that's leading to new momentum for voices and ideas to emerge in other media outlets. The more this happens, the more the stigma of "sympathizing with Russia" erodes. The best of these alternative ideas are now making it into the mainstream media.

What's needed next, of course, is for some publication like *The Atlantic* or *The New Yorker* to run a piece by Gorbachev or a retired member of The Elders – Jimmy Carter or Kofi Annan - on the need for peace in Ukraine. If the push for peace in Europe builds, that might finally convince the op-ed board of the *New York Times* to change its stance on Russia. And, more importantly, that would mark the ultimate mainstreaming of perspectives sympathetic to Russia's geopolitical concerns.

At the end of the day, logic and reason may win out in the marketplace of ideas over ideology and propaganda, and that's a good thing, whether you're in Washington or in Moscow. It means we're closer to ending the violence in Eastern Ukraine and coming up with a better security arrangement for a multi-polar world. The appearance of new ideas on Russia may not be able to change the macro view of how the world sees Russia, but it can at least help to avert a military catastrophe in Europe.

THE END

"The difficulty in understanding the Russian is that we do not take cognizance of the fact that he is not a European, but an Asiatic, and therefore thinks deviously. We can no more understand a Russian than a Chinaman or a Japanese, and from what I have seen of them, I have no particular desire to understand them, except to ascertain how much lead or iron it takes to kill them. In addition to his other Asiatic characteristics, the Russian has no regard for human life and is an all out son of bitch, barbarian, and chronic drunk."

- General George S. Patton, August 1945

Epilogue

In a move that caught foreign policy analysts by surprise, Russia has reorganized into two different sovereign countries. One country will continue to be known as Russia, and will hold all of the country's assets, corporations and organizations that have not been sanctioned by the West. The other country will henceforth be known as Rublestan and will comprise all of the country's sanctioned assets, corporations and organizations, including the nation's leading oil and gas companies. The new capital of Rublestan will be Rublyovka, the exclusive community outside of Moscow where many of the city's elite reside.

A Kremlin source, speaking under condition of anonymity, said the move was inspired by Google's unprecedented reorganization into a new company called Alphabet. "Our country is operating well today, but we think we can make it cleaner and more accountable," read the press release on the Kremlin's official website. "This new structure will allow us to keep tremendous focus on the extraordinary opportunities we have inside of Russia."

As a result of this move — the most sweeping reorganization of Russia since the breakup of the Soviet Union nearly 25 years ago — Russia will essentially become two different conglomerates of assets and companies. The country formerly known as Russia will be slimmed down to present a more favorable image to the West, while the new country of Rublestan will simply become a de facto holding company of the Kremlin.

One Western foreign policy analyst characterized this as a reorganization of Russia into "Good Russia" and "Bad Russia" brought about by the relentless appearance of Russophobia in the mainstream media. "Good Russia" will be a Western-leaning democracy filled with nongovernmental organizations, artists and a prosperous, Western-style middle class, while "Bad Russia" will be an authoritarian state filled with kleptocrats, arms dealers and massive, state-run corporations.

Notes

Introduction

Julia Ioffe, "The Remarkable Similarity of Putin's and Obama's Speeches at the UN," Foreign Policy, Sept. 29, 2015. http://foreignpolicy.com/2015/09/29/the-remarkable-similarity-of-putins-and-obamas-speeches-at-the-u-n/

Pavel Koshkin, "How Myths About Russia Embrace U.S. Identity," Russia Direct, August 23, 2013. http://www.russia-direct.org/qa/how-myths-about-russia-embrace-us-identity

Victoria Zhuravleva, "Understanding Russia in the United States: Images and Myths, 1881-1914," Kennan Institute, Wilson Center, November 18, 2013. https://www.wilsoncenter.org/event/understanding-russia-the-united-states-images-and-myths-1881-1914

Chapter One

Anna Arutunyan, "FIFA Corruption: Vladimir Putin Accuses U.S. of Meddling," USA Today, May 28, 2015. http://www.usatoday.com/story/sports/2015/05/28/putin-russia-fifa/28058777/

Dominic Basulto, "How Russia Views the Post-Cold War Global Order: Interview With Nicolai Petro," Russia Direct, October 27, 2014. http://www.russia-direct.org/qa/how-russia-views-post-cold-war-global-order

Ambrose Bierce, "The Devil's Dictionary," 1911.

Kate Brown, "From Russia to Hollywood: Find a New Bad Guy For Your Movies!" The Dotted Line Reporter, October 1, 2014. http://dlreporter.com/2014/10/01/russia-to-hollywod-find-a-new-bad-guy/

Stephen Castle, "A Russian TV Insider Describes a Modern Propaganda Machine," The New York Times, February 13, 2015. http://www.nytimes.com/2015/02/14/world/europe/russian-tv-insider-says-putin-is-running-the-show-in-ukraine.html

"Cover Trail: Russia's Sochi Olympics Price Tag," Bloomberg Businessweek, January 2, 2014. http://www.bloomberg.com/bw/articles/2014-01-02/sochi-winter-olympics-2014-the-making-of-bloomberg-businessweeks-cover

Alan Cowell, "Churchill's Definition of Russia Still Rings True," New York Times, August 1, 2008. http://www.nytimes.com/2008/08/01/world/europe/01iht-letter.1.14939466.html

"Crimea: The Way Home," Rossiya 1, documentary film, http://russia.tv/brand/show/brand_id/59195

Marquis de Custine, "Empire of the Tsar: A Journey Through Eternal Russia," 1839.

Miriam Elder, "'Nothing Is True and Everything Is Possible,' by Peter Pomerantsev," New York Times, Sunday Book Review, November 25, 2014. http://www.nytimes.com/2014/11/30/books/review/nothing-is-true-and-everything-is-possible-by-peter-pomerantsev.html

Mark Hay, "Is Russophobia a Thing?" GOOD Magazine, April 24, 2015. http://magazine.good.is/articles/russophobia

Rob Hornstra and Arnold van Bruggen, "An Atlas of War and Tourism in the Caucasus," Aperture, November 2013. http://aperture.org/shop/the-sochi-project-rob-hornstra-books

Stephen Kinzer, "Russia Is Not the Enemy," Boston Globe, September 20, 2015. https://www.bostonglobe.com/opinion/2015/09/19/russia-not-enemy/O0nCDUXrXAYLliutmqUtlN/story.html

"Henry Kissinger: The Interview," The National Interest, August 19, 2015. http://nationalinterest.org/feature/the-interview-henry-kissinger-13615

Pavel Koshkin, "How Myths About Russia Embrace U.S. Identity," Russia Direct, August 23, 2013. http://www.russia-direct.org/qa/how-myths-about-russia-embrace-us-identity

Sarah Lyall, "Got a Light? Olympic Torch Relay Seems Cursed to the Ends of the Earth," New York Times, December 17, 2013. http://www.nytimes.com/2013/12/18/sports/olympics/got-a-light-olympic-torch-relay-seems-cursed-to-the-ends-of-the-earth.html

Owen Matthews, "Is Russian Literature Dead?" Foreign Policy, March 24, 2015. http://foreignpolicy.com/2015/03/24/is-russian-literature-dead/

Russell O Phobe, "A Media Primer on the Art of Writing Russian Scare Stories," Russia Insider, September 15, 2015. http://russia-insider.com/en/media-criticism/media-primer-art-writing-russian-scare-stories/ri9725

Peter Pomerantsev, "Nothing Is True and Everything Is Possible: The Surreal Heart of the New Russia," Public Affairs, November 11, 2014.

Heather Schwedel, "Louis C.K. On His Miserable, Nihilistic Vacation to Post-Soviet Russia," New York Magazine, May 13, 2015. http://www.vulture.com/2015/05/louis-ck-talks-about-his-awful-trip-to-russia.html

Gary Shteyngart, "Out Of My Mouth Comes Unimpeachable Manly Truth," New York Times Magazine, February 18, 2015. http://www.nytimes.com/2015/02/22/magazine/out-of-my-mouth-comes-unimpeachable-manly-truth.html

George Soros, "Wake Up Europe," The New York Review of Books, November 20, 2014. http://www.nybooks.com/articles/archives/2014/nov/20/wake-up-europe/

Sputnik News, "Old Russophobia Lies at the Root of Modern Cold War Against Russia," August 14, 2015. http://sputniknews.com/politics/20150814/1025755003/russophobia-roots-cold-war.html

Sputnik News, "Russophobia for Dummies: How to Write Articles and Influence People," September 16, 2015. http://sputniknews.com/politics/20150916/1027102878/british-blogger-western-media-propaganda-anti-russia.html

Sputnik News, "Russophobia: Western Elite's Old Tool to Pressure Russia Into Submission," November 4, 2015. http://sputniknews.com/interviews/20151104/1029588079/russophobia-west-bolsheviks-stalin-russia.html

Paul Starobin, "The Eternal Collapse of Russia," The National Interest, August 28, 2014.
http://nationalinterest.org/feature/the-eternal-collapse-russia-11126

"Vladimir Putin's Legendary Speech at Munich Security Conference," YouTube, February 10, 2007.
https://youtu.be/ZlY5aZfOgPA

Chapter Two

Eugene Bai, "Putin's Orthodox Conservatives vs. Russia's Unorthodox Liberals," Russia Direct, January 20, 2015.
http://www.russia-direct.org/analysis/putins-orthodox-conservatives-vs-russias-unorthodox-liberals

Ty Burr, "Leviathan Masterfully Indicts Contemporary Russia," Boston Globe, February 19, 2015.
https://www.bostonglobe.com/arts/movies/2015/02/19/leviathan-masterfully-indicts-contemporary-russia/ADr0tVikz1qYl2LFDYcguO/story.html

Brendan Byrne, "Russia Building Arctic Bases In Preparation For World War 3? Value Walk, October 24, 2015.
http://www.valuewalk.com/2015/10/russia-building-arctic-bases-in-preparation-for-world-war-3/

Jonathan Chait, "The Pathetic Lives of Putin's American Dupes," New York Magazine, March 14, 2014.
http://nymag.com/daily/intelligencer/2014/03/pathetic-lives-of-putins-american-dupes.html

Robert Coalson, "How a Famous Soviet Dissident Foreshadowed Putin's Plan—in 1990," The Atlantic, September 2, 2014.

http://www.theatlantic.com/international/archive/2014/09/how-a-famous-soviet-dissident-foreshadowed-putins-planin-1990-russia-ukraine/379467/

Olga Doronina, "2014 for Russia – The Year No Experts Could Have Predicted," Russia Direct, December 25, 2014. http://www.russia-direct.org/analysis/2014-year-no-experts-could-have-predicted

Catherine A. Fitzpatrick, "The Boris Nemtsov Murder Conspiracy Theories," The Daily Beast, March 1, 2015. http://www.thedailybeast.com/articles/2015/03/01/who-killed-boris-nemtsov-a-rundown-of-the-conspiracy-theories.html

Alexander Gasyuk, "Thomas Graham: It's Time to Put the Cold War to Rest," Russia Direct, March 15, 2014. http://www.russia-direct.org/qa/thomas-graham-it%E2%80%99s-time-put-cold-war-rest

David E. Hoffman, "In 1983 War Scare, Soviet Leadership Feared Nuclear Surprise Attack by U.S.," Washington Post, October 24, 2015. https://www.washingtonpost.com/world/national-security/in-1983-war-scare-soviet-leadership-feared-nuclear-surprise-attack-by-us/2015/10/24/15a289b4-7904-11e5-a958-d889faf561dc_story.html

A.A. Indzhiev, "Battle for the Arctic: Will the North Be Russian?" Exmo, 2010. http://www.amazon.co.uk/Battle-Arctic-Russian-Arktiku-Russkim/dp/5699438262

Frank Jacobs, "What Russia Could Look Like in 2035, If Putin Gets His Wish," Foreign Policy, June 4, 2014.

http://foreignpolicy.com/2014/06/04/what-russia-could-look-like-in-2035-if-putin-gets-his-wish/

Joshua Keating, "Russian Government Blaming Islamists for Boris Nemtsov's Murder," Slate, March 9, 2015. http://www.slate.com/blogs/the_slatest/2015/03/09/russian_government_blaming_islamists_for_boris_nemtsov_s_murder.html

Mikhail Khodorkovsky, "Russia Under Putin and Beyond," Speech at Chatham House, Interpreter Magazine, February 26, 2015. http://www.interpretermag.com/russia-under-putin-and-beyond-mikhail-khodorkovskys-speech-at-chatham-house/

"Kompromat," New York Times, Sept. 30, 2009. http://schott.blogs.nytimes.com/2009/09/30/kompronat/?_r=0

Pavel Koshkin, "Will the Crimea Crisis Lead to Cold War II?" Russia Direct, March 7, 2014. http://www.russia-direct.org/analysis/will-crimea-crisis-lead-cold-war-ii

Mark Kramer, "Five Myths About the Cold War," Washington Post, March 13, 2014. https://www.washingtonpost.com/opinions/five-myths-about-the-cold-war/2014/03/13/e8f00f56-a4a5-11e3-84d4-e59b1709222c_story.html

Andrew Kuchins, "Is Putin Having a Brezhnev Moment?" Politico, March 11, 2014. http://www.politico.com/magazine/story/2014/03/putin-brezhnev-moment-crimea-104547#.UycYha1dUm5

Marlene Laruelle, "Russia's Arctic Strategies and the Future of the Far North," Routledge, January 2014.
http://www.amazon.com/gp/product/0765635011/

Maria Lipman, "How Russia Has Come to Loathe the West," European Council on Foreign Relations, March 13, 2015.
http://www.ecfr.eu/article/commentary_how_russia_has_come_to_loathe_the_west311346

Tim Marshall, "Russia and the Curse of Geography," The Atlantic, October 31, 2015.
http://www.theatlantic.com/international/archive/2015/10/russia-geography-ukraine-syria/413248/

Leon Neyfakh, "Putin's Long Game: Meet the Eurasian Union," Boston Globe, March 9, 2014.
http://www.bostonglobe.com/ideas/2014/03/09/putin-long-game-meet-eurasian-union/1eKLXEC3TJfzqK54elX5fL/story.html

"Putin as Warlord," Modern War Magazine, March/April 2015, Issue #16.
http://shop.strategyandtacticspress.com/ProductDetails.asp?ProductCode=MW16M

Philip Rucker, "Hillary Clinton Says Putin's Actions Are Like 'What Hitler Did Back in the '30s,'" Washington Post, March 5, 2014. http://www.washingtonpost.com/news/post-politics/wp/2014/03/05/hillary-clinton-says-putins-action-are-like-what-hitler-did-back-in-the-30s/

RIA Novosti, "Oliver Stone Open to Filming Documentary About Putin," Russia Beyond the Headlines, November 11, 2014.

http://rbth.com/news/2014/11/11/oliver_stone_open_to_filming_documentary_about_putin_41305.html

Russia Direct, "Eurasia: Russia's Link to Europe and Asia," March 14, 2014. http://www.russia-direct.org/archive/march-monthly-memo-eurasia-russias-link-europe-and-asia

David E. Sanger and Eric Schmitt, "Russian Ships Near Data Cables Are Too Close for U.S. Comfort," New York Times, October 25, 2015. http://www.nytimes.com/2015/10/26/world/europe/russian-presence-near-undersea-cables-concerns-us.html

Matthias Schepp and Gerald Traufetter, "Riches at the North Pole: Russia Unveils Aggressive Arctic Plans," Der Spiegel, January 29, 2009. http://www.spiegel.de/international/world/riches-at-the-north-pole-russia-unveils-aggressive-arctic-plans-a-604338.html

Zoe Schlanger, "The American Who Dared Make Putin's Case," Newsweek, March 10, 2014. http://www.newsweek.com/american-who-dared-make-putins-case-231388

Alexander Sergunin, "Has Putin the Pragmatist Turned Into Putin the Ideologue?" Russia Direct, April 14, 2014. http://www.russia-direct.org/analysis/has-putin-pragmatist-turned-putin-ideologue

Daisy Sindelar, "In Annals Of Russian Crime, North Caucasians Remain Popular Scapegoat," Radio Free Europe/Radio Liberty,

March 9, 2015. http://www.rferl.org/content/russia-north-caucasus-popular-scapegoat/26890029.html

Maria Snegovaya, "How Putin's Worldview May Be Shaping His Response in Crimea," Washington Post, March 2, 2014. https://www.washingtonpost.com/news/monkey-cage/wp/2014/03/02/how-putins-worldview-may-be-shaping-his-response-in-crimea/

Angela Stent, "Why America Doesn't Understand Putin," Washington Post, March 14, 2014. https://www.washingtonpost.com/opinions/why-america-doesnt-understand-putin/2014/03/14/81bc1cd6-a9f4-11e3-b61e-8051b8b52d06_story.html

Adam Taylor, "Russia's Deputy PM Tells U.S. Astronauts to Go to Space on a Trampoline," Washington Post, April 30, 2014. https://www.washingtonpost.com/news/worldviews/wp/2014/04/30/russias-deputy-pm-tells-u-s-astronauts-to-go-to-space-on-a-trampoline-the-joke-may-be-on-him/

Ukraine@War, "Analyzing the CCTV Footage That Seemed to Have Captured the Assassination of Boris Nemtsov," Feb. 28, 2015. http://ukraineatwar.blogspot.com/2015/02/analyzing-cctv-footage-that-seemed-to.html

Michael Wines, "Why Putin Boils Over: Chechnya Is His Personal War," New York Times, November 13, 2002. http://www.nytimes.com/2002/11/13/world/why-putin-boils-over-chechnya-is-his-personal-war.html

Sami Yousafzai, "A Taliban-Russia Team-Up Against ISIS?", The Daily Beast, October 26, 2015.

http://www.thedailybeast.com/articles/2015/10/26/a-taliban-russia-team-up-against-isis.html

Zero Hedge, "Russia Holds De-Dollarization Meeting: China, Iran Willing To Drop USD From Bilateral Trade," May 14, 2014. http://www.zerohedge.com/news/2014-05-13/russia-holds-de-dollarization-meeting-china-iran-willing-drop-usd-bilateral-trade

Chris Ziegler, "Liam Neeson Issues 'Taken'-Style Threat to Vladimir Putin on 'SNL'", The Verge, March 9, 2014. http://www.theverge.com/2014/3/9/5487664/liam-neeson-issues-taken-style-threat-to-vladimir-putin-on-snl

Chapter Three

Graham Allison and Dimitri K. Simes, "Russia and America: Stumbling Towards War," The National Interest, April 20, 2015. http://nationalinterest.org/feature/russia-america-stumbling-war-12662

Dominic Basulto, "Who Gets to Define What It Means to be Ukrainian?" Russia Direct, September 4, 2014. http://www.russia-direct.org/qa/who-gets-define-what-it-means-be-ukrainian

Leonid Bershidsky, "Putin in Syria Is Just Like Putin in Ukraine," Bloomberg View, October 1, 2015. http://www.bloombergview.com/articles/2015-10-01/putin-in-syria-is-just-like-putin-in-ukraine

Christopher Clark, "The Sleepwalkers: How Europe Went to War in 1914," Harper Perennial, March 2014.

http://www.amazon.com/Sleepwalkers-How-Europe-Went-1914/dp/0061146668/

Torie Rose DeGhett, "Russia Is Bombing a Lot of Familiar Faces in Syria," Vice News, October 14, 2015. https://news.vice.com/article/russia-is-bombing-a-lot-of-familiar-faces-in-syria

Michael Brendan Dougherty, "Yevgeny Zamyatin's 'We': A Dystopian Novel for the 21st Century." The Week, March 18, 2014. http://theweek.com/articles/449254/yevgeny-zamyatins-dystopian-novel-21st-century

Natan Dubovitsky, "Without the Sky," Russian Pioneer, March 12, 2014. http://ruspioner.ru/honest/m/single/4131

Mike Eckel, "Russia's Shock And Awe: Moscow Ups Its Information Warfare In Syria Operation," Radio Free Europe/Radio Liberty, October 7, 2015. http://www.rferl.org/content/russia-syria-shock-awe-military-air-strikes-information-warfare/27293854.html

Harold Evans, "On the Brink," New York Times (Sunday Book Review), May 9, 2013. http://www.nytimes.com/2013/05/12/books/review/the-sleepwalkers-and-july-1914.html?_r=0

Thomas Graham, "Europe's Problem Is With Russia, Not Putin," Financial Times, June 1, 2015. http://www.kyivpost.com/opinion/op-ed/thomas-graham-europes-problem-is-with-russia-not-putin-389970.html

Whitney Kassel, "Tupac in the Kremlin," Foreign Policy, March 20, 2014. http://foreignpolicy.com/2014/03/20/tupac-in-the-kremlin/

Andrew E. Kramer, et al. "Kremlin Says Russian 'Volunteer' Forces Will Fight in Syria," New York Times, October 5, 2015. http://www.nytimes.com/2015/10/06/world/europe/nato-russia-warplane-turkey.html?_r=1

"Piecing Together Guernica," BBC, April 7, 2009. http://news.bbc.co.uk/2/hi/uk_news/magazine/7986540.stm

Peter Pomerantsev, "How Putin is Reinventing Warfare," Foreign Policy, May 5, 2014. http://foreignpolicy.com/2014/05/05/how-putin-is-reinventing-warfare/

Yulia Ponomareva, "Papa Don't Preach: The McCain Sermon," Russia Direct, September 20, 2013. http://www.russia-direct.org/analysis/papa-don%E2%80%99t-preach-mccain-sermon

Zakhar Prilepin, "Sankya," Disquiet, April 29, 2014. http://www.amazon.com/Sankya-Zakhar-Prilepin/dp/1938604512

"War By Any Other Name," The Economist, July 5, 2014. http://www.economist.com/news/europe/21606290-russia-has-effect-already-invaded-eastern-ukraine-question-how-west-will

Chapter Four

Anna Arutunyan, "The Putin Mystique," Olive Branch Press, November 5, 2014. http://www.amazon.com/Putin-Mystique-Anna-Arutunyan/dp/1566569907

Dominic Basulto, "Everything You Need to Get Ready for Putin's Big UN Speech," Storify, Sept. 24, 2015. https://storify.com/dominicbasulto/everything-you-need-to-get-ready-for-putin-s-big-u

Bob Blaisell, "'The New Tsar' Traces the 'Rise and Reign' of Vladimir Putin," Christian Science Monitor, September 30, 2015. http://www.csmonitor.com/Books/Book-Reviews/2015/0930/The-New-Tsar-traces-the-rise-and-reign-of-Vladimir-Putin

Alexander Bratersky, "Report on Putin's Politburo 2.0 Sets Tongues Wagging," Moscow Times, August 22, 2012. http://www.themoscowtimes.com/news/article/report-on-putins-politburo-20-sets-tongues-wagging/466951.html

Rob Garver, "Why Donald Trump is Vladimir Putin's Favorite Presidential Candidate, " The Week, Oct. 9, 2015. http://theweek.com/articles/582178/why-donald-trump-vladimir-putins-favorite-presidential-candidate

Masha Gessen, "The Man Without a Face: The Unlikely Rise of Vladimir Putin," Riverhead Press, March 5, 2013. http://www.amazon.com/Man-Without-Face-Unlikely-Vladimir/dp/1594486514/

Thomas Graham, "A Russia Problem, Not a Putin Problem," Carnegie Perspectives on International Security, August 2014.

http://perspectives.carnegie.org/us-russia/a-russia-problem-not-a-putin-problem/

Mark Hensch, "Fiorina: Putin and Trump 'Have a Lot in Common'," The Hill, Sept. 22, 2015, http://thehill.com/blogs/ballot-box/presidential-races/254469-fiorina-putin-and-trump-have-a-lot-in-common

Fiona Hill and Clifford Gaddy, "Mr. Putin: Operative in the Kremlin," Brookings Institution Press, Feb. 2, 2015. http://www.amazon.com/gp/product/0815726171/

David Ignatius, "Is Donald Trump an American Putin?" Washington Post, August 18, 2015. https://www.washingtonpost.com/opinions/is-donald-trump-an-american-putin/2015/08/18/46c3dd38-45db-11e5-8ab4-c73967a143d3_story.html

Ben Judah, "Behind the Scenes in Putin's Court: The Private Habits of a Latter-Day Dictator," Newsweek, July 23, 2014. http://www.newsweek.com/2014/08/01/behind-scenes-putins-court-private-habits-latter-day-dictator-260640.html

Ben Judah, "Fragile Empire: How Russia Fell In and Out of Love with Vladimir Putin," Yale University Press, March 25, 2014. http://www.amazon.com/Fragile-Empire-Russia-Vladimir-Putin/dp/0300205228/

Manfred F.R. Kets de Vries and Stanislav Shekshnia, "Vladimir Putin, CEO of Russia Inc.," INSEAD working paper, 2005. http://www.insead.edu/facultyresearch/research/details_papers.cfm?id=15560

Andrei Korobkov, "Putin's UN Speech Showcases Russia's View of the Global Order," Russia Direct, Sept. 28, 2015. http://www.russia-direct.org/opinion/putins-un-speech-showcases-russias-view-shifting-global-order

Pavel Koshkin, "Why Russia's political elites need to play a more subtle game," Russia Direct, April 16, 2015. http://www.russia-direct.org/qa/why-russias-political-elites-need-play-more-subtle-game

Ivan Krastev and Gleb Pavlovsky, "What the West Gets Wrong About Russia," New York Times, August 12, 2015. http://www.nytimes.com/2015/08/13/opinion/what-the-west-gets-wrong-about-russia.html?_r=0

Evgeny Minchenko, "Politburo 2.0 and Post-Crimea Russia," Minchenko Consulting, 2014. http://www.minchenko.ru/en/analytics/analitics_9.html

Alexander Motyl, "Sex, Politics and Putin," World Affairs Journal, January 5, 2015. http://www.worldaffairsjournal.org/blog/alexander-j-motyl/sex-politics-and-putin

Steven Lee Myers, "The New Tsar: The Rise and Reign of Vladimir Putin," Knopf, September 29, 2015. http://www.amazon.com/New-Tsar-Reign-Vladimir-Putin/dp/0307961613/

Dmitry Polikanov, "Putin's UN Speech: Big on Ideas, Short on Details," Sept. 28, 2015. http://www.russia-direct.org/opinion/putin-un-speech-big-ideas-short-details

Vladimir Putin, Nataliya Gevorkyan, Natalya Timakova and Andrei Kolesnikov, "First Person: An Astonishingly Frank Self-Portrait by Russia's President," Public Affairs, May 2000, http://www.amazon.com/First-Person-Astonishingly-Self-Portrait-President/dp/1586480189/

Wess Roberts, "Leadership Secrets of Attila the Hun," Grand Central Publishing, 1990. http://www.amazon.com/Leadership-Secrets-Attila-Reprint-Roberts/dp/B00BXU64Q0/

RT, "Do You Realize What You've Done?' Putin Addresses UNGA 2015 (FULL SPEECH)," YouTube, Sept. 28, 2015. https://youtu.be/q13yzl6k6w0

Simon Shuster, "Inside Vladimir Putin's Circle," TIME, August 27, 2015. http://time.com/4012838/inside-vladimir-putins-circle/

Timothy Stanley and Alexander Lee, "It's Still Not the End Of History," The Atlantic, September 1, 2014. http://www.theatlantic.com/politics/archive/2014/09/its-still-not-the-end-of-history-francis-fukuyama/379394/

Richard Stengel, "Vladimir Putin: Person of the Year," TIME, December 19, 2007. http://content.time.com/time/specials/2007/personoftheyear/article/0,28804,1690753_1690757,00.html

Daniel Treisman, "Searching for the Roots of Russia's Aggression," Washington Post, September 25, 2015. https://www.washingtonpost.com/opinions/searching-for-the-roots-of-russias-aggression/2015/09/25/eede14a4-5713-11e5-b8c9-944725fcd3b9_story.html

Ivan Tsvetkov, "Russian Whataboutism vs. American Moralism," Russia Direct, August 26, 2014. http://www.russia-direct.org/opinion/russian-whataboutism-vs-american-moralism

"U.S. Pursues Double Standards By Backing Yemen's Hadi But Denying Support for Yanukovych – Lavrov," Russia Beyond the Headlines, March 27, 2015. http://rbth.com/news/2015/03/27/us_pursues_double_standa rds_by_backing_yemens_hadi_but_denying_support_f_44805.htm l

"Vladimir Putin: 2014 Person of the Year Runner-Up," TIME, December 2014. http://time.com/time-person-of-the-year-runner-up-vladimir-putin/

"Whataboutism," The Economist, January 31, 2008. http://www.economist.com/node/10598774

Chapter Five

Samuel Charap and Bernard Sucher, "Why Sanctions on Russia Will Backfire," New York Times, March 5, 2015. http://www.nytimes.com/2015/03/06/opinion/why-sanctions-on-russia-will-backfire.html?_r=1

"Development of Far East, Siberia 'National Priority' – Putin," Sputnik News/RIA Novosti, December 12, 2013. http://www.sputniknews.com/russia/20131212/185496942/D evelopment-of-Far-East-Siberia-National-Priority--Putin.html

Holly Ellyatt, "Why Siberia Could Be Russia's Secret Economic Weapon," CNBC, June 28, 2013. http://www.cnbc.com/id/100823089

Clifford Gaddy, "Russia's Development of Siberia: What Is To be Done," Brookings, June 18, 2013.
http://www.brookings.edu/blogs/up-front/posts/2013/06/18-siberia-russia-development-gaddy

Fiona Hill and Clifford Gaddy, "The Siberian Curse: How Communist Planners Left Russia Out In the Cold," Brookings Institution Press, November 4, 2003.
http://www.amazon.com/Siberian-Curse-Communist-Planners-Russia/dp/0815736452/

Sergey Karaganov, "Russia Needs One More Capital – In Siberia," Valdai Discussion Club, July 2, 2012.
http://valdaiclub.com/economy/45483.html

Anna Kuchma, "The Investment Climate in Siberia is Warming Up," Russia Direct, February 27, 2014. http://www.russia-direct.org/qa/investment-climate-siberia-warming

Chapter Six

Anastasia Borik, "Why a New Cold War Concerns Russian Top Thinkers," Russia Direct, May 1, 2014. http://www.russia-direct.org/analysis/why-new-cold-war-concerns-russian-top-thinkers

James Carden, "Neo-McCarthyism and the US Media," The Nation, May 19, 2015. http://www.thenation.com/article/neo-mccarthyism-and-us-media/

Chrystia Freeland, "The Rise of the New Global Elite," The Atlantic, January/February 2011.
http://www.theatlantic.com/magazine/archive/2011/01/the-rise-of-the-new-global-elite/308343/

Francis Fukuyama, "The End of History and the Last Man," Free Press, 1992. http://www.amazon.com/End-History-Last-Man/dp/0029109752/

"Jonathan Franzen Talks About His New Novel 'Purity', The National, June 1, 2015. http://www.thenational.ae/arts-lifestyle/books/author-jonathan-franzen-talks-about-his-new-novel-purity

"Jonathan Franzen's Top Ten List," The Top Ten: Writers Pick Their Favorite Books, http://www.toptenbooks.net/authors/jonathan-franzen

Pavel Koshkin, "The BRICS May Be Non-Western, But They Are Not Anti-Western," Russia Direct, July 10, 2015. http://www.russia-direct.org/qa/brics-may-be-non-western-they-are-not-anti-western

Pavel Koshkin, "The Paradox of Kremlin Propaganda: How It Tries to Win Hearts and Minds," Russia Direct, April 2, 2015. http://www.russia-direct.org/analysis/paradox-kremlin-propaganda-how-it-tries-win-hearts-and-minds

Pavel Koshkin, "The Sochi Opening Ceremony: Changing the Global Media's Opinion About the Olympics?", Russia Direct, February 10, 2014. http://www.russia-direct.org/analysis/sochi-opening-ceremony-changing-global-media%E2%80%99s-opinion-about-olympics

Pavel Koshkin, "Will the Crimea Crisis Lead to Cold War II?" Russia Direct, March 7, 2014. http://www.russia-direct.org/analysis/will-crimea-crisis-lead-cold-war-ii

Pavel Koshkin and Ksenia Zubacheva, "Are Kerry's Sochi Talks With Putin and Lavrov a Game-Changer?" Russia Direct, May 13, 2015. http://www.russia-direct.org/debates/are-kerrys-sochi-talks-putin-and-lavrov-game-changer

"Lavrov Gives Kerry Krasnodar Tomatoes, Potatoes and T-shirt; Kerry Gives Him List of Media Quotes," Russia Beyond the Headlines, May 12, 2015. http://rbth.com/news/2015/05/12/lavrov_gives_kerry_krasnodar_tomatoes_potatoes_and_t-shirt_kerry_gives_h_45928.html

Robert Legvold, "Managing the New Cold War," Foreign Affairs, June 16, 2014. https://www.foreignaffairs.com/articles/united-states/2014-06-16/managing-new-cold-war

Monocle, Soft Power Survey 2013, http://monocle.com/film/affairs/soft-power-survey-2013/

Portland Communications, The Soft Power 30: Digital Diplomacy Index, http://softpower30.portland-communications.com/ranking.

Russia Direct, "BRICS 2.0 and the Metamorphosis of Globalization," July 22, 2015. http://www.russia-direct.org/archive/russia-direct-brief-brics-20-and-metamorphosis-globalization

Gulnaz Sharafutdinova, "Here's Why Most Russia Experts Don't Get Russia," Russia Direct, May 7, 2014. http://www.russia-direct.org/opinion/here%E2%80%99s-why-most-russia-experts-don%E2%80%99t-get-russia

Dmitry Suslov, "How to Avoid a New Stagnation in the US-Russian Relationship," Russia Direct, Sept. 2, 2013.

http://www.russia-direct.org/analysis/how-avoid-new-stagnation-us-russian-relationship

Phillip Swarts, "Russian Ambassador to U.S.: Two Nations Must Work Together," Washington Times, June 16, 2014. http://www.washingtontimes.com/news/2014/jun/16/russian -ambassador-us-two-nations-must-work-togeth/

Artem Zagorodnov, "US-Russia Trade: Making Up For Lost Time," Russia Direct, June 15, 2013. http://www.russia-direct.org/qa/us-russia-trade-making-lost-time

Acknowledgements

In writing this book, I owe an immense debt of gratitude to all the wonderfully talented, creative and inspiring people that I've met in Moscow, St. Petersburg, Kiev and Sochi who have helped to shape my vision of the Russian world. I also owe a special thanks to my fellow Russophiles at Princeton and Yale who have inspired and encouraged me. And a special thanks to all my wonderfully talented colleagues at Russia Direct: Ekaterina, Pavel, Alexey, Ksenia and Olga.

About the author

Dominic Basulto is the U.S. Executive Editor of Russia Direct, which publishes news, analysis and reports about Russia, including most recently, "Insider's Guide to Russian High-Tech Hubs" and "Kremlin Lobbyists in the West."

He is the author of the first-ever iPad travel guide to Sochi, Russia and in 2014, he was a member of the Sochi 2014 Winter Olympics media and press operations team.

He currently lives in the New York City area, where he write about technology, innovation and Russian foreign policy. He has an MBA from Yale School of Management and an undergraduate degree in Politics and Russian Studies from Princeton.

www.ingramcontent.com/pod-product-compliance
Lightning Source LLC
Chambersburg PA
CBHW021615270326
41931CB00008B/715